Southern Living

Home for the
HOLIDAYS
Cookbook

Southern Living®

Home for the
HOLIDAYS
Cookbook

*Favorite holiday recipes and
easy decorating ideas*

Oxmoor
House®

CONTENTS

WELCOME

It should come as no surprise that the country's first Christmas celebrations began in the South. After all, in the South we take the traditions of the season quite seriously, building on cherished memories and adding charming new touches each year. And that's why we at *Southern Living* begin planning our holiday recipes and ideas during the hottest days of July. The temperatures inside our Test Kitchen match those outside with the heat of our ovens turning out batches of Christmas cookies and luscious cake layers.

Now we bring that quintessential Christmas experience to you. Start the season with our Holiday Guide on page 10 where some of the South's best decorators and hostesses share their secrets for fabulous style. Next, set a plan for a great holiday gathering with our Merry Starters, beginning on page 24, where you'll find great twists on your favorite Southern appetizers and beverages. Get inspiration for a memorable holiday dinner with some of our best entrées, starting on page 100 or a show-stealing side, from page 58 onward. And, of course, you'll want to end your meal with one of our sensational desserts, beginning on page 220.

Thank you for letting us share the holidays with you.

Warm wishes,

Susan

Susan Ray
EDITOR

HOLIDAY GUIDE

*Discover settings and centerpieces that will
make your seasonal table sparkle
with Southern charm*

WINTER WHITE

Subtle suggestions of the season—bare branches, fresh greenery, silver ornaments—play up the room's delicate air

THE SHELVES

From sparkly silver ornaments and wreaths to simple cut greenery and eucalyptus garlands, Betsy tucked festive flourishes in and around her everyday kitchen essentials to create a holiday tableau that looks effortless.

THE PLACE SETTING

Betsy's everyday-meets-fancy mix feels warm and inviting yet worthy of a special occasion. "Great contrasts make individual objects show up," she says. Here, the simplicity of restaurant-supply dinner plates and glazed terra-cotta salad plates allows the Baroque detailing of her Francis I silver flatware to stand out. Large Jacquard napkins folded underneath soften the bare table, while pencil-scrawled place cards supported by eucalyptus sprigs lend a casual, natural note.

THE TABLE AND CHAIRS

Made from three solid planks of reclaimed white oak, the 16-foot-long table, which doubles as Betsy's kitchen island, is 35 inches high—slightly lower than counter height but higher than table height. Ten white-lacquered barstools add slick contrast.

THE CENTERPIECE

A mix of shapes, textures, and heights adds drama without overpowering the room. Tall glass vases filled with cut branches create an unobstructive forest canopy, while squatty quadrants of square concrete vases filled with limes, hydrangeas, green hypericum berries and dusty miller add color. For a hint of holiday shine, Betsy scattered mercury glass balls.

MEET THE HOSTESS

BETSY BROWN

BIRMINGHAM, AL

IT'S CHRISTMAS WHEN...

I hang my daughters' white baby shoes on the tree. It makes me happier and sadder every year.

A DINING ROOM SHOULD BE...

In the center of the house with space for books, laptops, and cups of tea.

I NEVER... Use bows in my Christmas decor.

ON YOUR HOLIDAY PARTY

PLAYLIST: If I'm feeling modern, it's "White Christmas" by Bing Crosby, but if I want something classical, it's Bach's *Christmas Oratorio*.

ASSIGNED SEATS OR SIT

WHEREVER? Generally wherever, except for a few special occasions.

HOLIDAY DECOR GOES UP...

The week after Thanksgiving.

HOLIDAY DECOR COMES

DOWN... The day after Christmas.

SPARKLE IN SILVER

Inspired by the room's ethereal walls and the magnolia trees outside, designers Katie Collins and Martha Sweezey bring an everyday glamour to the table

THE ATMOSPHERE

This Dallas-based duo may spend their weekdays creating well-appointed interiors at their design firm, Collins & Sweezey, but in their off time, they are hostesses renowned for keeping their cool while putting together parties—especially holiday dinners. "We always want to create a relaxed but festive atmosphere that will surprise our guests," says Martha. To do so, they forgo the traditional red-and-green color scheme and use understated elements such as backyard greenery and mix-and-match china. "There's nothing better than a table roaring with laughter," Martha says, "and a beautiful setting and delicious food can really enhance that happy feeling."

THE PLACE SETTING

For a sentimental touch, Martha used her grandmother's formal salad plate (Raynaud's Si Kiang), but dinner is served on a basic stoneware plate from Wisteria. Bold green glassware accents the pear-colored charger, and a sprig of seeded eucalyptus livens up plain white linens. "A few key heirloom pieces give a table history," says Martha.

THE BAR

"I force amaryllis bulbs into bloom to get me in the Christmas spirit," says Martha. "They're a cinch to dress up with ribbons to fit the color scheme." Arranged in a punch bowl filled with ornaments, the flowers salute the bar, where the designers always set out a bottle of chilled Champagne and plenty of flutes for guests to serve themselves. "It's fun and easy," Katie says.

THE MANTEL

Carry your living room's Christmas decor into the dining room with accents such as a magnolia wreath and garland. "Greenery is both beautiful and accessible," says Martha, who scours her yard for ideas. Embellish the garland with elements from the tablescape such as gray brunia berries, boxwood clippings, mercury glass votives, and green ribbons to tie together the whole look.

THE PLACE CARDS

Calligraphy-adorned cards embossed with a laurel branch mark each seat. Though they seem formal, they simplify seating and make guests feel welcome. "It's a small detail to show you've thought about everything," says Martha.

MEET THE DESIGNERS

KATIE COLLINS AND MARTHA SWEEZEY

DALLAS, TX

RECTANGULAR OR ROUND DINING TABLE? Katie (above right): Round. It's more conducive to good conversation.

BEST CENTERPIECE: Martha: Magnolia branches arranged loosely in a silver Champagne bucket.

RECIPE FOR DISASTER: Leaving the three-onion gratin off the menu!

A SOUTHERN HOSTESS SHOULD ALWAYS... Martha: Use her heirlooms. During the holidays, it's a way to honor your family's history.

EVERY SOUTHERN HOSTESS SHOULD BE... Katie and Martha (in unison): Gracious.

YOUR FAVORITE CHRISTMAS TRADITION: Katie: Every year, our friends heat up their pool so the kids can swim. (Don't forget, we're in Texas!)

GOLDEN DAYS

Big doses of red, eclectic accessories, and glamorous gold make for an unabashedly festive table in a room designed with Christmas in mind

THE TABLE AND CHAIRS

Every element of Meg's dining room gets dressed up for Christmas dinner, and her seating setup is no exception. For a lavish focal point, she covers her 60-inch round table with a solid gold-hued skirt trimmed in red tassel fringe. She also swaps out her antique natural wooden chairs for gold-painted Chiavari versions that show up only for special occasions.

THE MANTEL

A symmetrical composition of red glass hurricanes flanking a gold sunburst mirror and a lush magnolia garland that swoops down below plays off the room's Classical architecture. Meg left the garland unadorned to emphasize its natural texture and wintry green-and-copper-hues.

THE CENTERPIECE

A single tightly bundled arrangement of amaryllis and garden roses makes for a showstopping splash of rich red in the middle of the table. The fluted brass container complements the bamboo detailing of Meg's flatware and chairs.

THE PLACE SETTING

Gilded chargers, Fitz and Floyd's Dragon Crest china, brass bamboo flatware, and ruby red stemware tie together Meg's holiday palette and penchant for Asian style. In keeping with the formal feel, calligraphed place cards rest in tasseled stands at each plate.

MEET THE HOSTESS

MEG BRAFF

TUPELO, MS

BEST DECORATING ADVICE: Measure twice, and never look back!

DINING ROOM ESSENTIAL: A big sideboard for buffet-style serving.

ENTERTAINING FAUX PAS: Clearing the dishes too soon.

IT'S CHRISTMAS WHEN... My husband makes a fuss picking out the perfect tree at our local lot.

BIGGEST HOSTESS COMPLIMENT: When a guest says, "I met so many nice people tonight."

ASSIGNED SEATS OR SIT WHEREVER? Assigned. Seating is key. I always try to put people with shared interests together.

ON YOUR HOLIDAY PARTY PLAYLIST: Any of Harry Connick, Jr.'s Christmas albums.

MERRY & BRIGHT

Reindeer candelabra, emerald accents, and mounds of blooms in sugarplum shades infuse designer Danielle Rollins' tailored, elegant room with holiday magic

THE TABLE AND CHAIRS

For a setup that accommodates a crowd and encourages lingering, Danielle paired an extra-long rectangular dining table with cushy French antique chairs upholstered in Champagne-hued silk. Contrasting blue piping and inset fabric tape add panache to the seats.

THE PALETTE

The serene ivory-and-aqua scheme in the dining room Danielle decorated with Miles Redd creates a neutral backdrop for any occasion. At Christmastime, she brings in flowers, votive holders, menus, and place cards in a festive mix of rich jewel tones and bold brights that really stand out.

THE HOLIDAY ACCENTS

Green glass votives and silver reindeer candelabra light up the table and lend a whimsical note to the otherwise traditional, formal setting. "These pieces are just plain fun and say Christmas to me," says Danielle.

THE PLACE SETTING

A few extra layers—malachite-patterned chargers, persimmon-hued menu cards, and ornament-appliquéd napkins—give holiday flair to Danielle's year-round Mottahedeh Tobacco Leaf china, Tiffany silver, and William Yeoward Crystal stemware. Hard candies in tiny vintage silver dishes sweeten the scheme and work as palate cleansers between courses.

THE CENTERPIECE

Blossoms in every celebratory shade but red—chartreuse and orange roses, magenta dahlias, and green hydrangeas—bring the design on Danielle's cachepots to life, while berries, bay leaves, and magnolia leaves add a nod to the season.

THE MANTEL

A few pheasant feathers plus leaves and pinecones are easy, luxe-looking additions to the simple magnolia garland bracing the fireplace.

THE PLACE CARDS

Danielle enlisted her childhood collection of Steinbach nutcrackers to hold place cards that match the menu cards. A gold foil holly sprig adorns both.

DANIELLE ROLLINS
ATLANTA, GA

BEST DECORATING LESSON LEARNED: Buy the best and you'll only cry once. It's better to wait and have it be perfect so you'll enjoy it for a lifetime.

ENTERTAINING FAUX PAS: Using paper napkins and serving food in takeout containers.

DINING ROOM ESSENTIALS: Life, laughter, conversation, clinking silver, and the aroma of good food.

IT'S CHRISTMAS WHEN: My total blend of family—both actual and acquired—are all gathered to celebrate.

BEST PARTY ICEBREAKER: A well-stocked bar!

ASSIGNED SEATS OR SIT WHEREVER? Assigned. I like to take out the guesswork for the guests.

ON YOUR HOLIDAY PARTY PLAYLIST: "Baby, It's Cold Outside."

PARTY-PREP MUST-HAVES: A glass of white wine, peppy music, and killer high heels.

HOLIDAY DECOR GOES UP... The day after Thanksgiving.

HOLIDAY DECOR COMES DOWN... On December 26.

MERRY STARTERS

Good friends and good food are a winning combination—especially during the holidays. This selection of appetizers and beverages makes any gathering more fun

Ham-and-Greens Crostini

Butternut Squash-and-Pecan Crostini

Pear-and-Blue Cheese Crostini, p. 28

Crostini

MAKES: 6 TO 8 SERVINGS HANDS-ON: 5 MIN. TOTAL: 15 MIN.

1 (8- to 10-oz.) French bread baguette, cut into ½-inch slices (35 to 40 pieces)

2½ Tbsp. extra virgin olive oil

Preheat oven to 400°. Place bread in a single layer on a baking sheet, and brush with olive oil. Bake 7 to 8 minutes or until lightly browned. Cool completely on a wire rack (about 2 minutes).

Ham-and-Greens Crostini

MAKES: 8 TO 10 APPETIZER SERVINGS HANDS-ON: 25 MIN.
TOTAL: 25 MIN., NOT INCLUDING CROSTINI

4 oz. country ham, finely chopped
2 Tbsp. olive oil
1 large bunch fresh collard greens (about 1½ lb.), washed, trimmed, and finely chopped
1 Tbsp. butter

⅛ tsp. ground red pepper
1 Tbsp. half-and-half
1 (8-oz.) goat cheese log, softened
Crostini (recipe above)

1. Cook ham in 1 Tbsp. hot oil in a large skillet over medium-high heat 3 to 4 minutes or until crisp. Remove from skillet using a slotted spoon, and drain on paper towels. Reserve drippings in skillet. Add greens and remaining oil to hot drippings in skillet; cook, stirring often, 4 to 5 minutes or until slightly wilted. Add butter and red pepper, and cook, stirring occasionally, 45 seconds. Stir in ham. Add salt and pepper to taste; transfer to a bowl.
2. Stir together half-and-half and goat cheese until smooth. Stir in half of greens mixture. Reserve remaining half of greens mixture.
3. Spread about 1 Tbsp. goat cheese mixture onto each Crostini. Top each with 1 tsp. reserved greens mixture.

Butternut Squash-and-Pecan Crostini

MAKES: 8 TO 10 APPETIZER SERVINGS HANDS-ON: 10 MIN.
TOTAL: 45 MIN., NOT INCLUDING CROSTINI

1 large butternut squash (about 1½ lb.), halved lengthwise and seeded
1 Tbsp. olive oil
½ tsp. smoked paprika
1 tsp. apple cider vinegar

2 Tbsp. butter, melted
Crostini (recipe above)
Shaved Parmesan cheese
¼ cup toasted pecans, chopped
Garnish: fresh sage leaves

MAKE AHEAD TIP

Chill the squash mixture up to 2 days. Microwave, stirring every 30 seconds, until hot.

1. Preheat oven to 425°. Place squash, flesh side up, in a 13- x 9-inch baking dish; drizzle with oil, and sprinkle with paprika. Add salt and pepper to taste. Turn squash, and place, flesh side down, in baking dish. Cover with heavy-duty aluminum foil. Bake 30 to 40 minutes or until tender. Cool in pan on a wire rack 5 minutes. Peel squash, and cut into large pieces.
2. Pulse squash, vinegar, and butter in a food processor 7 or 8 times or until smooth. Add salt and pepper to taste.
3. Spread 1 tsp. squash mixture onto each Crostini. Top each with a few pieces of shaved Parmesan and about ¼ tsp. pecans.

Pear-and-Blue Cheese Crostini

MAKES: **6 TO 8 APPETIZER SERVINGS** HANDS-ON: **10 MIN.**
TOTAL: **10 MIN., NOT INCLUDING CROSTINI**

1   ripe pear, thinly sliced
Crostini (recipe on page 27)
1   cup firmly packed baby arugula

4   oz. blue cheese, sliced
4   cooked bacon slices, coarsely chopped
Honey

Place 1 pear slice on each Crostini. Top with arugula, cheese, and bacon. Drizzle with honey.

Roquefort-Cognac Cheese Spread

*Inspired by a recipe from Julia Child, this sharp, tangy spread
can turn a celery stick into an unforgettable appetizer.*

MAKES: **ABOUT 1 ¼ CUPS** HANDS-ON: **10 MIN.** TOTAL: **2 HOURS 10 MIN.**

½   (8-oz.) package cream cheese, softened
¼   cup butter, softened
4   oz. Roquefort or other blue cheese, crumbled
1 ½ Tbsp. minced fresh chives
1   Tbsp. minced celery

1   Tbsp. cognac
⅛   tsp. ground red pepper
⅛   tsp. freshly ground pepper
Assorted crackers and sliced fresh vegetables

Beat cream cheese and butter at medium speed with a heavy-duty electric stand mixer until smooth. Beat in blue cheese and next 5 ingredients on low speed until blended. Spoon into a serving bowl. Chill 2 hours. Serve with crackers and vegetables.

Buttery Toasted Pecans

*Patiently roasting pecans (the entire 25 minutes!) at 325° to coax out
their flavor and essential oils takes them from good to great.*

MAKES: **4 CUPS** HANDS-ON: **10 MIN.** TOTAL: **35 MIN.**

¼   cup butter, melted
4   cups pecan halves

1   Tbsp. kosher salt
½   tsp. ground red pepper

Preheat oven to 325°. Toss together butter and pecans. Spread pecans in a single layer in a jelly-roll pan; bake 25 minutes or until toasted and fragrant, stirring halfway through. Remove from oven, and sprinkle with salt and pepper, tossing to coat. Cool completely. Store in an airtight container at room temperature up to 1 week.

Roquefort-Cognac Cheese Spread

Buttery Toasted Pecans

Citrus-Marinated
Olives and Almonds

Benne-Maple
Roasted Pecans

Citrus-Marinated Olives and Almonds

A big batch of this antipasto will last in the refrigerator up to a week. It's the perfect snack to serve unexpected holiday company. For extra flavor, use smoked almonds.

MAKES: **10 TO 12 APPETIZER SERVINGS** HANDS-ON: **10 MIN.** TOTAL: **4 HOURS 10 MIN.**

½ cup extra virgin olive oil
3 garlic cloves, crushed
2 Tbsp. loosely packed grapefruit zest
2 Tbsp. fresh grapefruit juice
2 Tbsp. red wine vinegar
1 Tbsp. chopped fresh thyme leaves
1 Tbsp. loosely packed orange zest

2 tsp. sugar
1 tsp. kosher salt
½ tsp. freshly ground black pepper
4 cups pitted and drained gourmet olives (such as Castelvetrano and kalamata)
1½ cups roasted salted almonds

1. Stir together first 10 ingredients in a large bowl. Fold olives into marinade. Cover and chill 4 to 24 hours.
2. Remove and discard crushed garlic cloves, and stir in almonds just before serving.

Benne-Maple Roasted Pecans

MAKES: **4 CUPS** HANDS-ON: **15 MIN.** TOTAL: **1 HOUR 5 MIN.**

¼ cup butter
4 cups pecan halves, toasted
¼ cup firmly packed light brown sugar
¼ cup maple syrup
¾ tsp. kosher salt

1 Tbsp. soy sauce
⅛ tsp. ground red pepper
1 Tbsp. sesame oil
Parchment paper
2 Tbsp. sesame seeds, toasted

1. Melt butter in a large saucepan over medium heat. Stir in pecans and next 5 ingredients. Cook over medium-high heat, stirring constantly, 5 minutes or until sugar dissolves and syrupy coating is almost evaporated. Stir in sesame oil; remove from heat.
2. Spread pecans in a single layer in a parchment paper-lined jelly-roll pan; sprinkle with sesame seeds. Cool completely.

Fried Hominy

MAKES: **8 TO 10 APPETIZER SERVINGS** HANDS-ON: **40 MIN.** TOTAL: **3 HOURS 45 MIN.**

2 (14.5-oz.) cans white hominy, drained
Canola oil
1 cup all-purpose flour
½ cup plain white cornmeal
¼ cup cornstarch

¾ tsp. table salt
½ tsp. freshly ground black pepper
Cinnamon-Sugar Spice Mix
Garnish: fresh thyme leaves

1. Spread hominy in a paper towel-lined jelly-roll pan; pat dry. Chill 3 to 24 hours. (Do not cover.) Heat 3 inches oil in a Dutch oven over medium-high heat to 350°. Mix flour and next 4 ingredients in a bowl. Toss hominy, in 2 batches, in flour mixture, shaking off excess.

2. Fry hominy, in 4 batches, stirring occasionally, 6 to 7 minutes or until kernels float to the top and begin to brown. Remove with a slotted spoon, and drain on paper towels. Immediately sprinkle with desired amount of Cinnamon-Sugar Spice Mix. Serve immediately, or cool completely, and store in an airtight container at room temperature up to 24 hours. Garnish, if desired.

Cinnamon-Sugar Spice Mix

Stir together ¼ cup granulated sugar, ¼ cup firmly packed light brown sugar, ¾ tsp. table salt, ¼ tsp. ground cinnamon, and ⅛ tsp. ground red pepper. Store in an airtight container up to 1 month. Makes about ½ cup.

Baked Brie

MAKES: **12 TO 14 APPETIZER SERVINGS** HANDS-ON: **40 MIN.** TOTAL: **1 HOUR 25 MIN.**

1 (8-oz.) Brie round
½ (16-oz.) package frozen phyllo pastry, thawed
Parchment paper
1 cup butter, melted
⅓ cup sweet orange marmalade

⅓ cup chopped fresh basil
¼ tsp. freshly ground black pepper
⅛ tsp. kosher salt
½ cup chopped roasted salted almonds, divided

1. Preheat oven to 375°. Trim and discard rind from sides of Brie. Cut Brie into ¼- to ½-inch slices. Place 2 phyllo pastry sheets side by side, long sides slightly overlapping, on parchment paper. (You should have an approximately 24- x 17-inch rectangle.) Brush with melted butter (4 to 5 brushes on each sheet). Top with 2 phyllo pastry sheets, and brush with butter. Repeat with butter and remaining ½ package of phyllo pastry sheets.

2. Arrange Brie slices across center of phyllo rectangle, overlapping slightly and leaving 3 ½ inches at each short end. Spread orange marmalade over Brie, and sprinkle with basil, pepper, salt, and ¼ cup chopped almonds. Fold phyllo into center, covering filling. (Long sides will overlap.) Carefully turn over phyllo packet, and place, seam side down, on parchment paper. Transfer phyllo packet and parchment paper to a baking sheet. Brush with remaining butter, and sprinkle with remaining ¼ cup almonds.

3. Bake at 375° for 30 to 40 minutes or until golden brown. Cool 15 minutes before slicing. Serve warm or at room temperature.

Benne-Maple
Roasted Pecans, p. 31

Fried Hominy

Blue Cheese-Walnut Wafers

Blue Cheese–Walnut Wafers

*Don't substitute margarine for butter in this recipe. The butter makes
these wafers wonderfully sweet and the dough easier to handle.*

MAKES: 4 DOZEN HANDS-ON: 20 MIN. TOTAL: 1 HOUR 40 MIN.

1 (4-oz.) package blue cheese, softened	1¼ cups all-purpose flour
½ cup butter, softened	⅓ cup finely chopped walnuts

1. Process first 3 ingredients in a food processor until smooth, stopping to scrape down sides. (Mixture will be sticky.) Spoon mixture into a bowl; stir in walnuts. Cover and chill 5 minutes.

2. Divide dough in half. Shape each portion into an 8-inch log. Wrap in heavy-duty plastic wrap; chill 1 hour.

3. Preheat oven to 350°. Slice dough into ¼-inch-thick slices; place on ungreased baking sheets. Bake 12 minutes or until lightly browned. Store in an airtight container up to a week.

Cheese Straws

MAKES: ABOUT 2 DOZEN HANDS-ON: 30 MIN. TOTAL: 1 HOUR 24 MIN.

1½ cups (6 oz.) shredded extra-sharp Cheddar cheese	½ tsp. kosher salt
¾ cup all-purpose flour	¼ to ½ tsp. dried crushed red pepper
¼ cup unsalted butter, cut into 4 pieces and softened	1 Tbsp. half-and-half

1. Preheat oven to 350°. Combine first 5 ingredients in a food processor; pulse in 5-second intervals until mixture resembles coarse crumbs. Add half-and-half, and process 10 seconds or until dough forms a ball.

2. Turn dough out onto a well-floured surface, and roll into an 8- x 10-inch rectangle (about ⅛ inch thick). Cut dough with a sharp knife into ¼- to ½-inch-wide strips, dipping knife in flour after each cut to ensure clean cuts. Place on ungreased baking sheets.

3. Bake at 350° for 12 minutes or until ends are slightly browned. Cool on baking sheets on a wire rack 30 minutes. Break into desired lengths.

MAKE AHEAD TIP

Freeze the baked cheese straws in a heavy-duty zip-top plastic freezer bag up to 3 months. Let thaw at room temperature 30 minutes before serving.

Chicken Liver Pâté

Serve this earthy, rustic spread with grilled bread and Cranberry-Pecan Chutney.

MAKES: 1 ½ CUPS HANDS-ON: 35 MIN. TOTAL: 6 HOURS 45 MIN.

1	lb. chicken livers, trimmed	2	Tbsp. butter, melted
2	cups milk	5	Tbsp. bourbon
4	bacon slices	1	tsp. kosher salt
2	garlic cloves, coarsely chopped	½	tsp. freshly ground black pepper
1	jalapeño pepper, seeded and chopped	2	Tbsp. butter, softened
½	tsp. finely chopped fresh thyme		Garnish: fresh thyme
½	tsp. finely chopped fresh rosemary		

1. Rinse livers, and pat dry with paper towels. Place livers in a large bowl, and add 1 cup milk; cover and chill 1 hour. Drain livers, and return to bowl. Add remaining 1 cup milk; cover and chill 1 hour. Drain livers, and pat dry with paper towels.

2. Cook bacon in a large skillet over medium heat 3 to 4 minutes on each side or until crisp. Drain on paper towels, reserving drippings in skillet. Finely chop bacon.

3. Cook livers, in batches, in hot drippings over medium heat 2 minutes on each side or until golden brown and done. Remove livers with a slotted spoon, and drain on paper towels. Discard drippings, and wipe skillet clean.

4. Sauté garlic, jalapeño, and next 2 ingredients in melted butter in skillet over medium-high heat 1 to 2 minutes or until fragrant. Stir in bourbon, salt and pepper; simmer 1 minute. Remove from heat, and cool 10 minutes.

5. Process livers, bacon, and garlic mixture in a food processor 60 to 90 seconds or until smooth. Add softened butter, and process 10 seconds or until blended. Transfer to a bowl; cover and chill 4 hours. Garnish, if desired.

Note: Chopped, cooked bacon may be omitted from the pâté and used as a topping instead, if desired.

Cranberry-Pecan Chutney

MAKES: 3 ½ CUPS HANDS-ON: 25 MIN. TOTAL: 1 HOUR

1	cup apple cider	½	tsp. whole cloves
¾	cup fresh orange juice	⅛	tsp. dried crushed red pepper
½	cup sugar	1	(12-oz.) package fresh or frozen cranberries
1	(3-inch) cinnamon stick	¾	cup dried apricots, diced
1	(1-inch) piece fresh ginger	½	tsp. loosely packed orange zest
½	tsp. kosher salt	½	cup chopped toasted pecans

1. Bring first 8 ingredients to a boil in a large saucepan over medium-high heat. Reduce heat to low, and simmer, stirring occasionally, 10 minutes. Remove cloves with a slotted spoon, and discard.

2. Add cranberries; increase heat to medium, and bring to a boil. Boil, stirring occasionally, 3 to 5 minutes or just until cranberries begin to pop. Discard cinnamon stick and ginger. Stir in apricots and orange zest; remove from heat. Cool completely. Serve immediately, or refrigerate in an airtight container up to 2 days. Stir in pecans just before serving.

Chicken Liver Pâté

Cranberry-Pecan Chutney

Warm Kale-and-Asiago Dip

MAKES: ABOUT 3 ½ CUPS   HANDS-ON: 35 MIN.   TOTAL: 1 HOUR 5 MIN.

5   bacon slices, chopped
1   lb. fresh kale, stemmed and finely chopped (about 1 bunch)
½   medium-size sweet onion, chopped
2   garlic cloves, chopped
¼   cup dry white wine
1   (8-oz.) package ⅓-less-fat cream cheese, softened
½   cup mayonnaise

1   cup plus 2 Tbsp. (4 ½ oz.) shredded Asiago cheese
1   cup plus 2 Tbsp. (4 ½ oz.) shredded Fontina or Swiss cheese
1   Tbsp. red wine vinegar
¼   to ½ tsp. dried crushed red pepper
¼   tsp. freshly ground black pepper
Assorted crackers and crudités

1. Preheat oven to 350°. Cook bacon in a Dutch oven over medium-high heat, stirring often, 6 to 7 minutes or until crisp; remove bacon, and drain on paper towels, reserving 1 Tbsp. drippings in Dutch oven. Sauté kale, onion, and garlic in hot drippings 7 to 8 minutes or until onion is tender. Add wine, and cook, stirring constantly, 1 to 2 minutes or until particles loosen from bottom of Dutch oven.
2. Lightly grease a 1- to 1½-qt. baking dish with cooking spray. Stir together cream cheese and mayonnaise in a large bowl until smooth. Stir in Asiago cheese, next 4 ingredients, and kale mixture. Spoon into baking dish.
3. Bake at 350° for 25 to 30 minutes or until center is hot and cheese is melted. Let stand 5 minutes; top with bacon. Serve with crackers and crudités.

MAKE AHEAD TIP

Prep recipe through Step 2. Cover and chill up to 24 hours. Let stand at room temperature for 30 minutes, and then bake.

Bacon and trendy kale update the usual hot spinach dip.

Cranberry-Goat Cheese Canapés

MAKE AHEAD TIP

Stir together the cranberry mixture up to 3 days ahead of time. Assemble the canapés the day of your party.

MAKES: 36 APPETIZER SERVINGS HANDS-ON: 25 MIN.
TOTAL: 55 MIN., INCLUDING TOAST SQUARES

1½ cups fresh cranberries, chopped	¾ tsp. grated fresh ginger
3 Tbsp. chopped fresh cilantro	Canapé Toast Squares (recipe below)
3 Tbsp. sugar	1 (5.3-oz.) container spreadable goat cheese
1½ Tbsp. minced fresh jalapeño pepper	

1. Stir together first 5 ingredients in a medium bowl. Let stand 10 minutes, stirring occasionally. Add salt and pepper to taste.
2. Spread each toast square with cheese, and top with a small spoonful of cranberry mixture.

Note: We tested with Chavrie Original Mild Goat Cheese.

Asparagus-Blue Cheese Canapés

MAKES: 36 APPETIZER SERVINGS HANDS-ON: 30 MIN.
TOTAL: 50 MIN., INCLUDING TOAST SQUARES

3 oz. Gorgonzola cheese, softened	1 large shallot, finely chopped
3 oz. cream cheese, softened	2 cups chopped fresh asparagus (8 oz.)
⅓ cup finely chopped toasted walnuts	Canapé Toast Squares (recipe below)
2 Tbsp. half-and-half	Garnish: lemon zest
2 Tbsp. butter	

1. Stir together first 4 ingredients in a small bowl.
2. Melt butter in a medium skillet over medium-high heat; add shallot, and sauté 2 minutes. Add asparagus, and sauté 2 minutes or just until crisp-tender. Add salt and pepper to taste.
3. Spread each toast square with cheese mixture, and top with asparagus mixture. Garnish, if desired.

Canapé Toast Squares

Preheat oven to 350°. Cut 9 square sandwich bread slices into 36 squares using a 2-inch square cutter. Place in a single layer on a baking sheet. Coat 1 side of bread slices with vegetable cooking spray. Bake 7 to 9 minutes or until lightly toasted. Makes 36 appetizer servings.

Note: We tested with Pepperidge Farm Original White and 100% Whole Wheat Stone Ground Bread.

Asparagus-Blue Cheese Canapés

Roasted
Shallot Dip

Rosemary Salt-and-
Vinegar Potato Chips

Roasted Shallot Dip

Caramelized sweet shallots and silky mascarpone cheese add new-school touches to onion soup dip. No need to waste time peeling all the shallots; after roasting, the papery skins easily slip away.

MAKES: ABOUT 4 CUPS HANDS-ON: 20 MIN. TOTAL: 5 HOURS 35 MIN.

1½ lb. shallots, unpeeled and root ends trimmed
3 garlic cloves, unpeeled
2 Tbsp. vegetable oil
1 (8-oz.) container sour cream
1 (8-oz.) container mascarpone cheese
⅓ cup thinly sliced fresh chives
1 Tbsp. fresh lemon juice

2 tsp. whole grain Dijon mustard
¾ tsp. kosher salt
½ tsp. freshly ground black pepper
Dash of hot sauce
Garnishes: cooked and crumbled bacon, lemon zest, chopped fresh chives

1. Preheat oven to 425°. Cut shallots in half. Toss together shallots and next 2 ingredients in a jelly-roll pan; add salt and pepper to taste. Bake 45 to 50 minutes or until shallots are light brown and skins are charred, stirring twice. Cool completely in pan on a wire rack (about 30 minutes). Remove and discard papery skins from shallots and garlic, and coarsely chop shallots and garlic.

2. Stir together sour cream and next 7 ingredients; fold in shallot mixture. Add salt and pepper to taste. Cover and chill 4 to 48 hours. Stir before serving. Add salt and pepper to taste just before serving, if desired. Garnish, if desired.

MAKE AHEAD TIP

Prepare recipe up to 2 days in advance; chill in an airtight container. Let stand at room temperture 30 minutes before serving.

Rosemary Salt-and-Vinegar Potato Chips

A homemade brine gives these chips a more delicate vinegar tang than mouth-puckering bagged varieties. They're the perfect chip for Roasted Shallot Dip.

MAKES: 6 APPETIZER SERVINGS HANDS-ON: 25 MIN. TOTAL: 25 MIN., PLUS 24 HOURS FOR CHILLING

2 cups malt or white vinegar
2 Tbsp. sugar
2 Tbsp. kosher salt, divided
2 large russet potatoes (about 2¼ lb.)

1 Tbsp. finely chopped fresh rosemary
1 tsp. freshly ground black pepper
Peanut oil

1. Combine vinegar, sugar, 1 Tbsp. salt, and 1 cup water in a medium-size glass bowl, stirring until sugar dissolves. Cut potatoes into thin slices, using a mandoline or sharp knife. (Cut them as thinly as you can.)

2. Stir potatoes into vinegar mixture; chill 24 hours.

3. Stir together rosemary, pepper, and remaining 1 Tbsp. salt in a small jar. Drain potatoes; gently pat dry with paper towels.

4. Pour oil to depth of 3 inches into a large Dutch oven; heat to 340°. Fry potatoes, in batches, stirring occasionally, 2 to 3 minutes or until golden brown. Drain on paper towels, and immediately sprinkle with rosemary mixture. Serve warm, or cool completely (about 10 minutes).

MAKE AHEAD TIP

Fry chips up to 1 day ahead, cool, and store in an airtight container. Re-crisp and warm the chips on a jelly-roll pan in a 300° oven for 20 to 25 minutes.

Pepper Jelly Palmiers

Prepare recipe through Step 1, and wrap the dough in plastic wrap. Freeze up to 1 month. Pick up with Step 2 about an hour before the party starts.

MAKES: ABOUT 4 DOZEN HANDS-ON: 20 MIN. TOTAL: 2 HOURS 10 MIN.

1 (17.3-oz.) package frozen puff pastry sheets, thawed
Parchment paper
1 cup plus 2 Tbsp. finely shredded Parmesan cheese
6 Tbsp. chopped fresh chives
½ tsp. kosher salt
½ tsp. freshly ground black pepper
½ cup hot pepper jelly
Garnish: chopped fresh chives

1. Roll 1 pastry sheet into a 12- x 10-inch rectangle on lightly floured parchment paper. Sprinkle with half of cheese, 3 Tbsp. chives, and ¼ tsp. each salt and pepper. Roll up pastry, jelly-roll fashion, starting with each short side and ending at middle of pastry sheet. Wrap pastry tightly with parchment paper. Repeat procedure with remaining pastry sheet, cheese, chives, salt, and pepper. Freeze pastries 1 to 24 hours.
2. Preheat oven to 375°. Remove pastries from freezer, and let stand at room temperature 10 minutes. Cut each roll into ¼-inch-thick slices, and place on parchment paper-lined baking sheets.
3. Bake, in batches, at 375° for 20 minutes or until golden.
4. Microwave pepper jelly in a microwave-safe bowl at HIGH 1 minute. Spread ½ tsp. pepper jelly onto each palmier. Garnish, if desired. Serve immediately.

Traditional party staples, pepper jelly and puff pastry, go uptown in this flaky, sweet-and-savory pastry.

Pimiento Cheese Gougères

Pimiento Cheese Gougères

Stamp a Southern accent on this classic French hors d'oeuvre. You can use a piping bag with a ½-inch round tip or a zip-top plastic freezer bag with a corner snipped off to pipe the dough rounds onto the baking sheets. This tasty treat pairs nicely with jam or preserves.

MAKES: ABOUT 4 ½ DOZEN HANDS-ON: 35 MIN. TOTAL: 1 HOUR 45 MIN.

½	cup butter, cut up	1 ½	cups (6 oz.) finely shredded sharp Cheddar cheese
¾	tsp. kosher salt	1 ½	tsp. Dijon mustard
1 ¼	cups all-purpose flour	¼	tsp. ground red pepper
1	(4-oz.) jar diced pimiento, drained		Parchment paper
4	large eggs		

1. Preheat oven to 425°. Bring first 2 ingredients and 1 cup water to a boil in a 3-qt. saucepan over medium heat; cook, stirring constantly, 1 minute. Add flour all at once, and beat vigorously with a wooden spoon 1 minute or until mixture is smooth and pulls away from sides of pan, forming a ball of dough. Reduce heat to low, and cook, stirring constantly, 2 minutes. (Dough will begin to dry out.) Remove from heat, and let stand 5 minutes.

2. Meanwhile, pat pimiento dry with paper towels, and finely chop.

3. Add eggs to dough, 1 at a time, stirring until blended after each addition. (If dough separates, don't worry. It will come back together.) Add pimiento, cheese, and next 2 ingredients; stir 2 minutes or until fully combined.

4. Drop half of dough by level tablespoonfuls 1 inch apart onto 2 parchment paper-lined baking sheets.

5. Bake at 425° for 10 minutes, placing 1 baking sheet on middle oven rack and other on lower oven rack. Reduce temperature to 325°, switch baking sheets, and bake 10 to 12 more minutes or until golden and crisp. Cool on baking sheets 5 minutes. Repeat procedure with remaining dough. Serve warm.

MAKE AHEAD TIP

Freeze completely cooled gougères in a zip-top freezer bag up to 1 month. To reheat, place frozen gougères on baking sheets, cover loosely with aluminum foil, and bake at 350° for 10 minutes or until warm.

Mushroom Canapés

MAKES: ABOUT 3 DOZEN HANDS-ON: 30 MIN. TOTAL: 2 HOURS 30 MIN.

2	Tbsp. butter	1	tsp. lemon juice
1	(8-oz.) package fresh mushrooms, chopped	¼	tsp. garlic powder
1	(8-oz.) package cream cheese, cubed and softened	⅛	tsp. hot sauce
1	Tbsp. dry white wine	16	(½-inch-thick) white bread slices

1. Melt butter in a skillet; add mushrooms, and sauté 10 minutes or until liquid has evaporated.

2. Process cream cheese and next 4 ingredients in a blender or food processor until smooth, stopping to scrape down sides. Stir in sautéed mushrooms; chill at least 2 hours.

3. Cut bread slices with a 2- or 2 ½-inch shaped cutter. Spread mushroom mixture on bread.

Sesame Salmon Croquettes

MAKE AHEAD TIP

Prepare the recipe as directed. Cool completely, and freeze in zip-top plastic bags. Bake at 350° for 10 to 15 minutes or until warm.

MAKES: ABOUT 3 ½ DOZEN HANDS-ON: 45 MIN. TOTAL: 1 HOUR 45 MIN.

1	lemon
2	Tbsp. kosher salt
1	(1-lb.) salmon fillet
2 ½	cups panko (Japanese breadcrumbs), divided
2	large eggs
2	green onions, thinly sliced
¼	cup chopped fresh cilantro
¼	cup mayonnaise
2	tsp. loosely packed lime zest

2	Tbsp. fresh lime juice
1	Tbsp. finely grated fresh ginger
1	(1.62-oz.) jar toasted sesame seeds
2	garlic cloves, minced
½	tsp. kosher salt
¼	tsp. freshly ground black pepper
⅓	cup butter, melted
	Ginger Rémoulade (recipe on page 51)

1. Cut lemon in half. Squeeze juice from lemon into a 3-qt. saucepan. Add lemon halves, 2 Tbsp. salt, and 6 cups water, and bring to a boil over medium-high heat. Add salmon fillet (cut into 2 pieces, if necessary); cover and reduce heat to low. Simmer 4 minutes. (Center of salmon will be raw.) Carefully transfer salmon to a large bowl, and cool completely (about 10 minutes). Remove and discard skin from salmon, and flake salmon.

2. Preheat oven to 425°. Stir ½ cup panko and next 11 ingredients into flaked salmon.

3. Lightly grease a 24-cup miniature muffin pan with cooking spray. Stir together melted butter and remaining 2 cups panko. Spoon 1 tsp. panko mixture into each cup of muffin pan. Add 1 Tbsp. salmon mixture to each muffin cup. Top each with 1 tsp. panko mixture.

4. Bake, in batches, at 425° for 10 minutes or until topping is golden brown. Serve warm with Ginger Rémoulade.

Black-Eyed Pea Pâté

MAKES: 4 CUPS HANDS-ON: 25 MIN. TOTAL: 45 MIN., PLUS 8 HOURS FOR CHILLING

1 ½	cups frozen black-eyed peas
½	jalapeño pepper, seeded
¾	cup chopped country ham
1	(3.5-oz.) package fresh shiitake mushrooms, sliced (or 4 oz. sliced button mushrooms)
3	garlic cloves, chopped
½	cup olive oil, divided

¼	cup dry white wine
½	cup finely chopped toasted walnuts
½	cup finely chopped fresh flat-leaf parsley
2	tsp. chopped fresh thyme
	Pickled Red Onions and Cukes (recipe below), drained
	Crostini (recipe on page 27)

1. Cook peas according to package directions, adding jalapeño to water. Drain.

2. Sauté ham and next 2 ingredients in 2 Tbsp. hot olive oil over medium-high heat 4 to 5 minutes or until lightly browned. Stir in wine, and cook, stirring occasionally, 1 minute.

3. Process peas, jalapeño, ham mixture, and remaining 6 Tbsp. olive oil in a food processor just until smooth. Stir in walnuts and next 2 ingredients; add salt and pepper to taste. Cover and chill 8 to 24 hours.

4. Stir pâté, and add salt and pepper to taste. Transfer to a shallow bowl, or spoon into small jars. Top with desired amount of Pickled Red Onions and Cukes. Serve with Crostini.

Pickled Red Onions and Cukes

Stir together ½ medium-size red onion, thinly sliced; ½ English cucumber, seeded and sliced; 1 cup seasoned rice wine vinegar; 1 garlic clove, minced; ¼ cup water; 1 Tbsp. sugar; and 1 ½ tsp. table salt in a large bowl. Cover and chill 2 hours to 2 days. Makes about 1 ½ cups.

Sesame Salmon
Croquettes

**Shrimp Cocktail
with Avocado Cream**

Ginger Rémoulade

Mexican Shrimp Cocktail Dip

MAKES: 8 TO 10 APPETIZER SERVINGS HANDS-ON: 30 MIN. TOTAL: 1 HOUR 30 MIN.

1 lb. peeled, medium-size cooked shrimp, deveined and halved	¼ cup chili sauce
3 plum tomatoes, diced	¼ cup spicy tomato juice
3 jalapeño peppers, seeded and diced	2 Tbsp. hot sauce
1 small sweet onion, diced	2 Tbsp. prepared horseradish
1 garlic clove, minced	¼ cup chopped fresh flat-leaf parsley
½ cup fresh lime juice	¼ cup chopped fresh cilantro
¼ cup extra virgin olive oil	1 avocado, diced
	Tortilla chips

1. Stir together first 13 ingredients in a bowl. Cover and chill 1 to 24 hours.

2. Stir in avocado; add salt and pepper to taste. Serve with tortilla chips.

Shrimp Cocktail

MAKES: 12 SERVINGS HANDS-ON: 10 MIN. TOTAL: 25 MIN., INCLUDING CREAM AND RÉMOULADE

3 lb. peeled, large cooked shrimp with tails	Ginger Rémoulade (recipe below)
Avocado Cream (recipe below)	

Place shrimp on a serving platter; serve with either or both of the sauces.

Avocado Cream

Scoop pulp from 1 large avocado into a medium bowl, and mash until very smooth. Stir in 1 (8-oz.) container sour cream, 2 Tbsp. chopped fresh dill weed, 2 Tbsp. chopped fresh flat-leaf parsley, 1 tsp. loosely packed lemon zest, 2 Tbsp. fresh lemon juice, and 1 green onion, minced. Add salt and pepper to taste. Serve immediately, or refrigerate in an airtight container up to 1 day. Stir well before serving. Garnish with dill sprig, if desired. Makes 1 ¾ cups.

Ginger Rémoulade

Stir together 1 cup mayonnaise, 2 minced green onions, 2 Tbsp. Asian chili-garlic sauce, 1 Tbsp. whole grain Dijon mustard, 1 Tbsp. fresh lime juice, and 4 tsp. grated fresh ginger. Add salt and pepper to taste. Serve immediately, or refrigerate in an airtight container up to 3 days. Stir well before serving. Makes 1 ⅓ cups.

Mini Corn Cakes with Smoked Salmon and Dill Crème Fraîche

Make these in the morning, and top with salmon and crème fraîche just before your guests arrive. Tight on time? Use store-bought blini instead.

MAKES: ABOUT 4 DOZEN HANDS-ON: 20 MIN. TOTAL: 1 HOUR 10 MIN.

1	(8.25-oz.) can cream-style corn	1	cup crème fraîche
1	cup plain white cornmeal	2	Tbsp. finely chopped fresh dill weed
1	cup sour cream	1	Tbsp. fresh lemon juice
2	Tbsp. vegetable oil	2	(4-oz.) packages thinly sliced smoked salmon, flaked
1½	tsp. baking powder		
1	tsp. table salt		Garnish: fresh dill weed
2	large eggs		

1. Preheat oven to 350°. Grease a 24-cup miniature muffin pan well with vegetable cooking spray. Whisk together first 7 ingredients until smooth. Spoon 1 heaping teaspoonful corn mixture into each cup of muffin pan.

2. Bake, in batches, at 350° for 20 minutes. Cool 10 minutes.

3. Stir together crème fraîche, dill, and lemon juice. Top muffins with crème fraîche and salmon. Garnish, if desired.

Cheese Dreams

These little gems will be the first appetizer to disappear. Make them the day before and refrigerate, or freeze up to 3 weeks. If frozen, pop in the oven straight from the freezer; increase the bake time by 10 minutes.

MAKES: ABOUT 3 DOZEN HANDS-ON: 30 MIN. TOTAL: 45 MIN.

2	cups finely grated sharp Cheddar cheese	½	tsp. table salt
1	cup butter, softened	½	tsp. dry mustard
2	Tbsp. heavy cream		Ground red pepper or hot sauce to taste
1	large egg	1	(16-oz.) package firm white sandwich bread slices
1	tsp. Worcestershire sauce		

1. Preheat oven to 375°. Beat cheese and butter at medium speed with an electric mixer until blended. Beat in cream and next 5 ingredients.

2. Lightly grease a baking sheet with cooking spray. Cut crusts from bread slices; cut each bread slice into 4 squares. Spread cheese mixture on half of bread squares (about 1 tsp. per square); top each with 1 remaining square. Spread remaining cheese mixture over top and sides of sandwiches. Place sandwiches, 1 inch apart, on baking sheet.

3. Bake at 375° for 15 minutes or until golden brown.

Note: We tested with Pepperidge Farm White Sandwich Bread.

Cheese
Dreams

Mini Corn Cakes with
Smoked Salmon and
Dill Crème Fraîche

Montgomery Punch

Montgomery Punch

MAKES: 14 CUPS HANDS-ON: 15 MIN. TOTAL: 9 HOURS 40 MIN., INCLUDING ICE RING

2 cups fresh lemon juice	1 (375-milliliter) bottle chilled dessert wine (such as Sauternes)
1½ cups sugar	
1 cup brandy	Garnishes: orange slices, lemon slices, cranberries
Ice Ring (recipe below)	
2 (750-milliliter) bottles chilled sparkling wine	

Stir together first 2 ingredients until sugar dissolves. Stir in brandy. Pour over Ice Ring in a punch bowl. Stir in sparkling and dessert wines. Garnish, if desired.

Ice Ring

Freeze 3 cups water in a tube pan or Bundt pan (able to fit into a punch bowl) 4 hours or until set. Place sliced fruit, such as lemons and oranges, in a single layer over ice, and freeze 1 hour. Remove from freezer; let stand 10 minutes. Add 5 cups ice-cold water; freeze 4 hours or until set. Let stand at room temperature 10 minutes before unmolding. Makes 1 ice ring.

Bloody Marys by the Pitcher

A great Bloody Mary is a must-have at brunch for some of us. Rather than make several cocktails one by one in glasses, why not stir them up by the pitcher? If your guests cannot agree on an amount of vodka, or perhaps want none at all, omit it from the base recipe and serve it on the side.

MAKES: 1 ½ QT. HANDS-ON: 10 MIN. TOTAL: 10 MIN.

46 oz. low-sodium vegetable juice, chilled	1 Tbsp. Worcestershire sauce
1 Tbsp. freshly ground black pepper	½ tsp. Old Bay seasoning
3 Tbsp. fresh lime juice	½ cup vodka, chilled
1 Tbsp. hot sauce	Ice cubes

1. Stir together vegetable juice, pepper, lime juice, hot sauce, Worcestershire, and Old Bay in a large pitcher.
2. Stir in vodka and serve over ice.

Milk Punch

Not everyone has had a chance to enjoy a delicious milk punch. It is served cold and usually has nutmeg sprinkled on top. It is similar to eggnog, but less rich. At least one batch of Milk Punch is traditional on holidays throughout the Deep South and remains a popular brunch beverage in New Orleans.

MAKES: ABOUT 5 CUPS HANDS-ON: 10 MIN. TOTAL: 10 MIN.

2   cups milk
2   cups half-and-half
1   cup brandy or bourbon
½   cup sifted powdered sugar

1 ½   tsp. vanilla extract
Crushed ice
Freshly grated nutmeg

1. Whisk together milk, half-and-half, brandy, powdered sugar, and vanilla in a pitcher.
2. Serve over crushed ice. Top each serving with freshly grated nutmeg.

Julian's Old Fashioned

Many of us associate the Van Winkle family with some of the best bourbon in the world. We can trust Julian's precise advice on making an old-fashioned cocktail.

MAKES: 1 SERVING HANDS-ON: 10 MIN. TOTAL: 10 MIN.

1 to 2 brown sugar cubes
2 to 3 drops orange bitters
2 to 3 drops Angostura bitters

1   fresh orange slice
1 ½ to 2 oz. bourbon
Ice cubes

1. Place brown sugar cubes on a cocktail napkin. Sprinkle orange bitters and Angostura bitters over sugar cubes. (Napkin will soak up excess bitters.) Transfer cubes to a 10-oz. old-fashioned glass.
2. Add orange slice and a few drops bourbon to glass. Mash sugar cubes and orange slice, using a muddler, until sugar is almost dissolved. (Avoid mashing the rind, which can release a bitter flavor.)
3. Add 1 ½ to 2 oz. bourbon, and fill glass with ice cubes. Stir until well chilled. Add more bourbon, if desired.

Milk Punch

SEASONAL SIDES & SALADS

Any of these tasty dishes will be the perfect complement to your holiday meal

Citrus Salad with Spiced Honey

MAKES: 6 TO 8 SERVINGS HANDS-ON: 30 MIN. TOTAL: 1 HOUR 5 MIN.

½	cup honey
1	(3-inch) cinnamon stick
1	bay leaf
1	tsp. black peppercorns*
¼	tsp. dried crushed red pepper
4	whole cloves
3	medium-size oranges

3	mandarin oranges
2	Ruby Red grapefruit
2	limes
6	kumquats (optional)
1	(4.4-oz.) package fresh pomegranate seeds

Toppings: extra virgin olive oil, fresh mint leaves, sea salt

1. Bring first 6 ingredients and ½ cup water to a boil in a saucepan over medium-high heat. Boil, stirring often, 1 minute. Remove from heat, and let stand 30 minutes.

2. Meanwhile, peel oranges, next 3 ingredients, and, if desired, kumquats. Cut away bitter white pith. Cut each fruit into thin rounds. Arrange on a serving platter, and sprinkle with pomegranate seeds.

3. Pour honey mixture through a fine wire-mesh strainer, discarding solids. Drizzle fruit with desired amount of spiced honey; reserve remaining spiced honey for another use (such as flavoring iced tea). Top with a drizzle of olive oil, fresh mint leaves, and sea salt.

* Pink or red peppercorns may be substituted.

Note: Salad may be made up to a day ahead. Prepare as directed; cover and chill up to 24 hours.

Use any combination of sweet and tart citrus fruit on hand to compose this vibrant, fresh salad, and present it however you like. No matter how you serve it, sweet and sunny citrus brightens any roast or fish.

Citrus-Kale Salad

Use your favorite citrus for this refreshing salad. We love the colorful mix and flavor combination of two navel oranges, one blood orange, and Ruby Red grapefruit. No matter what fruit you choose, buy an extra navel orange to juice for the dressing.

MAKES: 8 TO 10 SERVINGS HANDS-ON: 30 MIN. TOTAL: 30 MIN.

3	large oranges	1	tsp. honey
2	Ruby Red grapefruit	½	tsp. freshly ground black pepper
3	Tbsp. fresh orange juice	¼	cup extra virgin olive oil
2	Tbsp. white wine vinegar	1	(5-oz.) package baby kale
2½	tsp. Dijon mustard	½	cup thinly sliced red onion
1	tsp. sugar	1	(3-oz.) goat cheese log or feta cheese, crumbled
1	tsp. kosher salt		

1. Peel oranges and grapefruit; cut away bitter white pith. Cut each orange into ¼-inch-thick rounds. Holding 1 peeled grapefruit in the palm of your hand, slice between membranes, and gently remove whole segments. Repeat with remaining grapefruit.

2. Whisk together orange juice and next 6 ingredients. Add oil in a slow, steady stream, whisking constantly until smooth. Toss together kale, onion, and ½ cup dressing in a large bowl. Add salt and pepper to taste. Top salad with citrus, and sprinkle with cheese. Serve with remaining dressing.

Bloody Mary Green Bean Salad

We turned a festive cocktail into a salad by making the drink's crunchy garnishes (green beans and celery) the stars and dressing them with a vinaigrette made with Zing Zang Bloody Mary Mix.

MAKES: 6 TO 8 SERVINGS HANDS-ON: 35 MIN. TOTAL: 35 MIN.

SALAD

1	lb. haricots verts (French green beans), trimmed
½	cup thinly sliced red onion
12	pickled okra pods, sliced
1	pt. grape tomatoes, halved
4	celery ribs, sliced
¼	cup fresh celery leaves

DRESSING

⅓	cup Bloody Mary mix (such as Zing Zang)
2	Tbsp. fresh lemon juice
1½	tsp. dry mustard
¾	tsp. kosher salt
¾	tsp. hot sauce (such as Tabasco)
¼	tsp. ground black pepper
4½	tsp. prepared horseradish, divided
½	cup extra virgin olive oil

1. Prepare Salad: Cook beans in boiling salted water to cover 2 minutes or until crisp-tender; drain. Plunge into ice water; drain and pat dry. Combine beans, onion, and okra in a large bowl. Combine tomatoes, celery, and celery leaves in a separate bowl.

2. Prepare Dressing: Whisk together Bloody Mary mix, next 5 ingredients, and 4 tsp. of horseradish in a medium bowl. Add oil in a slow, steady stream, whisking constantly until blended.

3. Toss bean mixture with ¼ cup dressing; arrange on a platter. Stir remaining ½ tsp. horseradish into ¼ cup dressing, and toss with tomato mixture. Spoon tomato mixture over bean mixture. Add salt and pepper to taste; serve with remaining dressing.

Citrus-Kale Salad

Brussels Sprouts Salad with Hot Bacon Dressing

MAKES: **6 SERVINGS** HANDS-ON: **1 HOUR** TOTAL: **1 HOUR**

2   lb. fresh Brussels sprouts
1   large red apple (such as Honeycrisp), thinly sliced
5   smoked bacon slices, cut into ½-inch pieces
½   cup apple cider vinegar
1   Tbsp. Dijon mustard
1   tsp. kosher salt

2   tsp. honey
½   tsp. ground black pepper
1   cup thinly sliced red onion
½   cup olive oil
1½   Tbsp. fresh lemon juice
1   tsp. sugar

1. Remove and discard stem ends from Brussels sprouts; peel leaves, and place in a large bowl. Add apple slices.

2. Place bacon in a single layer in a large cold skillet. Cook bacon over medium heat 4 to 5 minutes on each side or until crisp. Remove bacon, reserving drippings in skillet. Add cooked bacon to Brussels sprouts mixture.

3. Add vinegar to skillet, and bring to a boil over medium heat, stirring to loosen browned bits from bottom of skillet. Boil 1 minute or until reduced to about ⅓ cup, stirring occasionally.

4. Stir in mustard and next 4 ingredients. Add oil in a slow, steady stream, stirring constantly, until blended. Remove from heat, and stir in lemon juice and sugar. Pour hot dressing over Brussels sprouts mixture; toss. Add salt and pepper to taste; serve immediately.

*Whole Brussels sprout leaves make beautiful little salad greens.
If pressed for time, slice the sprouts instead of peeling.*

Kale-and-Collards Salad

When making this bracing salad, dress the kale and collards in advance to tenderize them.

MAKES: 8 TO 10 SERVINGS HANDS-ON: 30 MIN.
TOTAL: 1 HOUR 35 MIN., INCLUDING LEMON DRESSING

8	oz. fresh collard greens		2	avocados, diced
8	oz. fresh Tuscan kale		1	Tbsp. fresh lemon juice
¾	cup sweetened dried cranberries		1	small head radicchio, shredded
Lemon Dressing (recipe below)			¾	cup chopped toasted pecans
3	Bartlett pears, sliced		6	bacon slices, cooked and crumbled

1. Trim and discard tough stalks from centers of collard and kale leaves; stack leaves, and roll up, starting at 1 long side. Cut into ¼-inch-thick slices. Toss collards and kale with cranberries and Lemon Dressing in a large bowl. Cover and chill 1 hour.

2. Toss together pears and next 2 ingredients just before serving. Toss pear mixture, radicchio, pecans, and bacon with collard mixture. Serve immediately.

Lemon Dressing

¼	cup fresh lemon juice		1	tsp. kosher salt
2	garlic cloves, minced		½	tsp. freshly ground black pepper
2	tsp. Dijon mustard		½	cup olive oil

Whisk together lemon juice, garlic, Dijon mustard, kosher salt, and freshly ground black pepper in a small bowl. Add olive oil in a slow, steady stream, whisking constantly until smooth. Makes about 1 cup.

A Mess of Greens

MAKES: 8 TO 10 SERVINGS HANDS-ON: 25 MIN. TOTAL: 2 HOURS 30 MIN.

2	Tbsp. butter		3	(1-lb.) packages fresh collard greens, washed, trimmed, and cut into thin strips
3	Tbsp. olive oil			
1	small sweet onion, diced		¼	to ½ cup diced jarred jalapeño peppers, drained (optional)
1	Tbsp. minced garlic cloves			
1	(12 oz.) smoked ham hock		Pepper sauce	

1. Melt butter with oil in a large Dutch oven over medium-high heat. Add onion, and sauté 5 minutes or until lightly browned. Add garlic; sauté 1 minute. Add ham hock, and gently stir.

2. Add half of collards and 2 cups water. Cover and cook over medium-high heat, stirring occasionally, 10 minutes. Add remaining collards and 8 cups water; bring to a boil. Cover, reduce heat to low, and simmer 2 hours. Stir in jalapeño peppers, if desired. Add salt and black pepper to taste, and serve with pepper sauce.

Kale-and-Collards
Salad

Fall Salad with Beets and Apples

MAKES: **6 TO 8 SERVINGS** HANDS-ON: **35 MIN.** TOTAL: **5 HOURS**

1   lb. red or yellow beets, peeled and thinly sliced into half moons
½   cup white balsamic vinegar
½   cup white wine vinegar
5   Tbsp. honey
2   tsp. kosher salt
½   medium-size sweet onion, cut into thin strips
½   cup extra virgin olive oil
2   Tbsp. white wine vinegar

1   tsp. spicy brown mustard
6   thick applewood-smoked bacon slices, cooked and crumbled
1   (8 oz.) Gala apple, thinly sliced
3   cups firmly packed baby arugula
3   cups loosely packed frisée, torn
½   cup loosely packed fresh flat-leaf parsley leaves
¼   cup toasted chopped walnuts

1. Place beets and water to cover in a microwave-safe bowl; microwave at HIGH 8 to 10 minutes or until crisp-tender. Let stand 30 minutes. Drain and rinse beets.

2. Stir together ½ cup white balsamic vinegar, next 3 ingredients, and 2 Tbsp. water; pour into a large zip-top plastic freezer bag. Add beets and onion. Seal and chill 4 hours.

3. Drain beets and onion, reserving ⅓ cup pickling liquid. Discard remaining liquid. Whisk together olive oil, next 2 ingredients, and reserved ⅓ cup pickling liquid until smooth. Add salt and pepper to taste. Toss together bacon, next 5 ingredients, and desired amount of dressing. Serve with beets, onion, and remaining dressing.

Perfectly balanced with seasonal flavors, textures, and colors, this salad is a colorful addition to a fall spread.

Root Vegetable Mash

MAKE AHEAD TIP

You can peel your potatoes a day in advance. Just drop the peeled potatoes in a bowl of cold water and add a small amount of lemon juice. Cover and store in the refrigerator overnight.

1 garlic bulb
1 large rutabaga (about 1 lb.), peeled and cut into 1-inch cubes
1 lb. celery root, peeled and cut into 1-inch cubes
3 large russet potatoes (about 2 ½ lb.), peeled and quartered

¾ cup milk
¼ cup unsalted butter
1 ½ tsp. freshly ground black pepper
1 tsp. kosher salt
1 Tbsp. thinly sliced fresh chives (optional)

1. Preheat oven to 425°. Cut off pointed end of garlic bulb; place bulb on a piece of aluminum foil. Fold to seal. Bake 30 minutes; cool 10 minutes.

2. Meanwhile, bring rutabaga, celery root, and salted water to cover to a boil in a Dutch oven; boil 15 minutes or until tender. Drain. Bring potatoes and salted water to cover to a boil in a 4-qt. saucepan; boil 15 minutes or until tender. Drain. Combine rutabaga mixture and potatoes in Dutch oven.

3. Heat milk in a small saucepan over low heat 3 to 5 minutes or until thoroughly heated.

4. Add butter, next 2 ingredients, and hot milk to vegetable mixture. Squeeze pulp from 2 roasted garlic cloves into mixture; reserve remaining garlic for another use. Mash vegetable mixture with a potato masher until light and fluffy. (Use a food processor for a silkier texture.) Add chives, if desired. Serve immediately.

Whipped, tender root vegetables and creamy roasted garlic elevate the typical mash. Any root will do.

Sautéed Mushrooms

Sautéed Mushrooms

Any types of mushrooms work well here. Sear them in batches, without crowding, in a hot skillet so that they will take on color without steaming.

MAKES: 8 SERVINGS HANDS-ON: 35 MIN. TOTAL: 35 MIN.

1   (8-oz.) package stemmed and sliced fresh shiitake mushrooms
4 ½ Tbsp. olive oil
2   large portobello mushrooms (about 8 oz.), stemmed, cleaned, and chopped
1   (8-oz.) package stemmed and sliced oyster mushrooms*

2   Tbsp. butter
3   Tbsp. minced shallots
2   garlic cloves, chopped
½   tsp. kosher salt
½   tsp. freshly ground black pepper
1   Tbsp. sliced fresh chives

1. Cook shiitake mushrooms in a single layer in 1 ½ Tbsp. hot oil in a 10- to 12-inch nonstick skillet over high heat, stirring often, 4 to 6 minutes or until browned. Transfer to a medium bowl. Repeat procedure two more times with portobello mushrooms, oyster mushrooms, and remaining oil.

2. Melt butter in skillet over medium-high heat; add shallots, and sauté 2 to 3 minutes or until tender. Stir in garlic; cook 1 minute. Add mushrooms, salt, and pepper; toss gently to coat. Remove from heat; stir in chives. Serve warm.

* Cremini or button mushrooms may be substituted.

Stuffing-Stuffed Onions

Hollow out and fill roasted onions with a chunky stuffing for a twist on the hearty casserole version.

MAKES: 8 SERVINGS HANDS-ON: 45 MIN. TOTAL: 2 HOURS

8   small yellow onions (about 2 ¼ lb.)
1 ½ cups organic chicken broth, divided
½   cup butter, divided
2   celery ribs, thinly sliced
¼   cup finely chopped fresh flat-leaf parsley

1   Tbsp. finely chopped fresh sage
2 ½ cups fresh French breadcrumbs, toasted
1   tsp. kosher salt
½   tsp. freshly ground black pepper
Garnish: fresh sage leaves

1. Preheat oven to 425°. Cut a thin slice from bottom (rounded end) of each onion, forming a base for onions to stand. Cut ½ inch from sprout end of each onion, and discard. Peel onions. Remove and reserve center of each onion, leaving 2 layers of onion as a thick shell. Finely chop 1 cup reserved onion centers. Reserve remaining onion centers for another use, if desired.

2. Place hollowed onions in a 2-qt. baking dish, and add 1 cup broth. Cut 2 Tbsp. butter into 8 pieces, and place 1 piece in each onion. Cover with aluminum foil, and bake at 425° for 25 to 30 minutes or until shells are tender. Remove from oven to a wire rack, and cool 20 minutes.

3. Pour liquid from onions into a measuring cup, and add broth (about ¼ cup) to equal 1 cup. Reduce oven temperature to 350°.

4. Melt 4 Tbsp. butter in a large skillet over medium-high heat; add celery and 1 cup chopped onion, and sauté 5 minutes or until tender. Stir in parsley and sage, and cook, stirring constantly, 1 minute or until fragrant. Stir in breadcrumbs, salt, pepper, and 1 cup reserved broth mixture. Remove from heat.

5. Fill hollowed onions with stuffing, and place in a shallow 9-inch baking dish or pie plate. Add remaining ¼ cup broth to pan. Bake at 350° for 30 to 35 minutes or until stuffing is golden brown and thoroughly heated. Transfer to a serving platter. Stir remaining 2 Tbsp. butter into cooking liquid, and spoon over onions. Garnish, if desired.

Roasted Root Vegetables

Use any 4-lb. combo of hardy root vegetables to make this simple side.

MAKES: 6 SERVINGS   HANDS-ON: 30 MIN.   TOTAL: 1 HOUR 45 MIN.

1	lb. turnips	½	cup olive oil
1	lb. rutabagas	2	Tbsp. chopped fresh rosemary
1	lb. carrots	2	tsp. kosher salt
1	lb. parsnips	1	tsp. black pepper
3	shallots, halved	8	garlic cloves

Preheat oven to 400°. Peel first 4 ingredients; cut into 1-inch pieces. (If your carrots are small enough, leave them whole.) Toss with shallots and next 4 ingredients. Place in a single layer in a 17- x 11-inch jelly-roll pan. Bake 30 minutes, stirring halfway through. Add garlic; bake 45 minutes or until tender, stirring at 15-minute intervals.

Note: You can prepare this recipe 4 hours ahead. Cool in pan 30 minutes or to room temperature; bake at 450° for 10 to 15 minutes or until hot.

Corn Pudding

Take one bite of this rich custard, and you'll include it on your holiday menu for years to come.

MAKES: 8 SERVINGS   HANDS-ON: 25 MIN.   TOTAL: 1 HOUR 25 MIN.

½	cup unsalted butter	3	Tbsp. chopped fresh basil
5	cups fresh yellow corn kernels	1	Tbsp. sugar
1	cup diced yellow onion	1	Tbsp. kosher salt
4	large eggs	¾	tsp. freshly ground black pepper
1	cup milk	1	cup (4 oz.) shredded extra-sharp
1	cup half-and-half		Cheddar cheese, divided
1	cup softened goat cheese		

1. Preheat oven to 350°. Melt butter in a large skillet over medium-high heat; add corn and onion, and sauté 4 minutes. Remove from heat, and cool 10 minutes.

2. Meanwhile, whisk together eggs and next 2 ingredients in a large bowl; gradually whisk in goat cheese until blended. Whisk in basil and next 3 ingredients; stir in corn mixture and ¾ cup Cheddar cheese until blended. Lightly grease a 2-qt. baking dish with cooking spray. Spoon corn mixture into baking dish; sprinkle with remaining ¼ cup Cheddar cheese.

3. Bake at 350° for 40 to 45 minutes or until golden brown and a knife inserted in center comes out clean. Remove from oven to a wire rack, and cool 15 minutes.

Corn Pudding

Roasted Root
Vegetables

Stuffing-Stuffed
Onions, p. 73

Southern Giardiniera

MAKES: 12 TO 14 SERVINGS HANDS-ON: 30 MIN.
TOTAL: 1 HOUR 30 MIN., PLUS 1 DAY FOR STANDING

1 lb. multicolored baby carrots with tops	1 Tbsp. black peppercorns
4 cups apple cider vinegar	1 (10-oz.) package fresh red pearl onions, peeled and halved
1½ cups granulated sugar	
1 cup firmly packed light brown sugar	2 cups small fresh broccoli florets
½ cup kosher salt	2 jalapeño peppers, sliced
⅓ cup molasses	1 (8-oz.) package sweet mini peppers
1½ Tbsp. yellow mustard seeds	1 medium-size fresh fennel bulb, sliced

1. Trim tops from carrots, leaving 1 inch of greenery on each; peel carrots. Cut carrots in half lengthwise. Bring vinegar, granulated sugar, brown sugar, salt, molasses, mustard seeds, and peppercorns to a boil in a medium-size nonaluminum saucepan over medium-high heat, stirring until sugars and salt dissolve. Reduce heat to medium; add carrots and onions, and simmer 3 minutes, stirring occasionally.

2. Place broccoli and next 3 ingredients in a large heatproof bowl; pour hot vinegar mixture over vegetables. Cool completely (about 1 hour). Stir occasionally while mixture cools.

3. Transfer vegetables to 2 hot sterilized 1-qt. jars, using a slotted spoon and filling to 1 inch from top. Pour cooled vinegar mixture from bowl into a liquid measuring cup with a pour spout. Pour enough vinegar mixture into jars to cover vegetables, and discard remaining vinegar mixture. Cover with metal lids, and screw on bands. Let stand 24 hours before using. Refrigerate in an airtight container up to 2 weeks.

Set these bread-and-butter-style pickled veggies out on your relish tray so guests can nosh on them before and during dinner. Red pearl onions add vibrant color to the relish, but white onions will work, too.

Collard Greens Gratin

MAKES: 6 TO 8 SERVINGS HANDS-ON: 35 MIN. TOTAL: 2 HOURS 30 MIN.

5	cups heavy cream	2	(1-lb.) packages chopped collard greens
3	garlic cloves, minced	8	bacon slices, diced
2	cups freshly grated Parmigiano-Reggiano cheese, divided	2	cups chopped yellow onion
1	tsp. cornstarch	½	cup panko (Japanese breadcrumbs)
		1	Tbsp. olive oil

1. Preheat oven to 350°. Bring first 2 ingredients to a boil over medium-high heat. Reduce heat to low, and simmer 30 minutes or until reduced by half. Stir in 1 cup cheese.

2. Stir together cornstarch and 1 Tbsp. water. Whisk into cream mixture until thickened.

3. Cook collards in boiling salted water to cover 5 to 7 minutes or until tender; drain and pat dry with paper towels. Cool 10 minutes; coarsely chop.

4. Cook bacon in a large skillet over medium-high heat, stirring often, 8 to 10 minutes or until crisp. Add onion, and cook 5 minutes or until tender. Stir in collard greens, and cook, stirring constantly, 3 minutes. Stir in cream mixture. Add salt and pepper to taste.

5. Lightly grease a 2-qt. baking dish with cooking spray. Pour collard mixture into baking dish. Stir together panko, olive oil, and remaining 1 cup cheese; sprinkle over collard mixture.

6. Bake at 350° for 35 to 40 minutes or until breadcrumbs are golden brown. Let stand 5 minutes before serving.

Move over, creamed spinach—there's a new steak house side in town. Give packaged collards an extra chop with a sharp knife to get them to bite-size pieces.

Sweet Potato
Soldiers

Savory Bacon-and-Leek
Bread Pudding

Savory Bacon-and-Leek Bread Pudding

We love how buttery Gouda and nutty Parmesan lend richness and depth of flavor to this dish.

MAKES: 6 TO 8 SERVINGS   HANDS-ON: 40 MIN.   TOTAL: 1 HOUR 20 MIN.

8 large eggs, lightly beaten	6 cups cubed challah bread (1-inch cubes)
1 cup half-and-half	1¼ cups grated Gouda cheese, divided
1 cup heavy cream	1¼ cups freshly grated Parmesan cheese, divided
2 tsp. kosher salt	2 leeks
1 tsp. dried thyme	2 Tbsp. butter
1 tsp. dried marjoram	2 garlic cloves, minced
1 tsp. ground black pepper	8 cooked bacon slices, crumbled

1. Preheat oven to 350°. Whisk together first 7 ingredients in a large bowl; stir in bread cubes and 1 cup each Gouda and Parmesan cheeses.

2. Remove and discard root ends and dark green tops of leeks. Cut in half lengthwise, and rinse thoroughly under cold running water to remove grit and sand. Thinly slice.

3. Lightly grease an 11- x 7-inch baking dish or individual ramekins with cooking spray. Melt butter in a medium skillet over medium heat. Add leeks, and cook, stirring occasionally, 7 to 8 minutes or until tender. Add garlic, and cook, stirring constantly, 1 minute. Fold leek mixture and bacon into egg mixture. Pour into baking dish or ramekins. Sprinkle with remaining ¼ cup each Gouda and Parmesan cheeses.

4. Bake at 350° for 35 to 40 minutes or until center is set. Let stand 5 minutes.

Sweet Potato Soldiers

MAKES: 6 SERVINGS   HANDS-ON: 40 MIN.   TOTAL: 1 HOUR 35 MIN.

2 lb. small fingerling sweet potatoes (6 [7- x 1½-inch] potatoes), unpeeled	¼ cup honey
½ cup fresh orange juice	2 Tbsp. dark rum or bourbon
¼ cup butter	½ tsp. ground ginger
¼ cup firmly packed light brown sugar	1 Tbsp. butter
	Sea salt

1. Preheat oven to 425°. Pierce potatoes several times with a fork. Arrange in a single layer in a jelly-roll pan, and bake 25 to 35 minutes or until just tender. Transfer to a wire rack; cool completely (about 30 minutes).

2. Meanwhile, bring orange juice and next 5 ingredients to a simmer in a small saucepan over medium-low heat. Simmer, stirring often, 5 minutes or until thickened. Remove from heat.

3. Peel sweet potatoes, and cut crosswise into 1½-inch pieces, discarding ends.

4. Melt 1 Tbsp. butter in a 10-inch cast-iron skillet; cook over medium heat 1 minute or until butter begins to brown. Carefully add sweet potatoes, cut sides down, and cook 5 minutes. (Do not stir; move the skillet across the cooking eye to promote even browning.)

5. Pour orange juice mixture over potatoes, and cook 10 minutes or until glaze is slightly thickened. Transfer potatoes, seared sides up, to a serving platter; pour glaze over potatoes, and sprinkle with salt.

MAKE AHEAD TIP

Prepare as directed through Step 2. Place potatoes in a zip-top plastic freezer bag and glaze in an airtight container; refrigerate up to 3 days. Reheat glaze in a saucepan over medium heat 10 minutes. Proceed as directed in Steps 3 through 5.

Roasted Squash with Farro and Almonds

*Look for farro, a grain gaining in popularity, in your supermarket,
or substitute wild rice. High in fiber, farro's firm texture and nutty flavor pair well
with tender, sweet roasted squash and creamy crumbles of cheese.*

MAKES: 6 TO 8 SERVINGS HANDS-ON: 25 MIN. TOTAL: 1 HOUR 35 MIN.

1	cup uncooked farro	¼	cup roasted unsalted almonds, chopped
½	small butternut or kabocha squash, peeled	3	Tbsp. balsamic vinegar
	and cut into ½-inch pieces (about 2 lb.)	2	Tbsp. honey
¼	tsp. kosher salt	⅛	tsp. ground red pepper
¼	tsp. ground cinnamon	1	shallot, minced
⅛	tsp. ground nutmeg	2	cups chopped radicchio or Belgian endive
⅛	tsp. ground black pepper	1	cup loosely packed fresh flat-leaf parsley leaves
6	Tbsp. olive oil, divided	3	oz. crumbled blue cheese (optional)

1. Lightly grease 2 jelly-roll pans with cooking spray. Bring 6 cups salted water to a boil in a Dutch oven over high heat. Add farro, and boil, stirring occasionally, 25 to 30 minutes or until tender. Drain farro, and spread in a single layer in 1 jelly-roll pan. Chill, uncovered, 30 minutes.

2. Meanwhile, preheat oven to 450°. Toss together squash, next 4 ingredients, and 2 Tbsp. olive oil in a large bowl. Spread squash in a single layer in second jelly-roll pan, and bake 10 to 15 minutes or just until tender. Cool in pan 30 minutes.

3. Stir together almonds, next 4 ingredients, and remaining ¼ cup olive oil in a small bowl. Add salt to taste. Let stand 10 minutes.

4. Stir together farro, radicchio, and parsley in a medium bowl. Spoon desired amount of almond vinaigrette over farro; toss to coat. Transfer to a serving platter. Top with roasted squash and, if desired, blue cheese. Serve with remaining vinaigrette.

Carrot-Cauliflower Salad

We created this crunchy, sweet side as an update of the classic mayonnaise-laden carrot-and-raisin salad. Save time and make it ahead—it tastes even better the next day.

MAKES: 8 SERVINGS HANDS-ON: 30 MIN.
TOTAL: 1 HOUR 10 MIN., INCLUDING VINAIGRETTE

2 **lb. carrots, thinly sliced**	**Orange Vinaigrette (recipe below)**
2 **(6-oz.) packages baby rainbow carrots, diagonally sliced**	1 **cup loosely packed fresh flat-leaf parsley leaves**
1 **Tbsp. kosher salt**	½ **cup toasted walnuts, coarsely chopped**
2 **Tbsp. apple cider vinegar**	⅓ **cup chopped dried dates**
1 **lb. fresh cauliflower, cut into small florets**	2 **oz. feta cheese, crumbled**

1. Toss together first 4 ingredients; drain in a colander 30 minutes.

2. Meanwhile, cook cauliflower in boiling salted water to cover, stirring occasionally, 1 to 2 minutes or until crisp-tender; drain. Rinse under cold running water until cool; drain.

3. Rinse carrots under cold running water; drain and pat dry. Toss together carrots, cauliflower, Orange Vinaigrette, and remaining ingredients in a large bowl. Add salt to taste. Serve immediately.

Note: To make ahead, dress carrots and cauliflower with vinaigrette, but toss with parsley, walnuts, dates, and cheese just before serving.

Orange Vinaigrette

Orange Vinaigrette replaces mayonnaise in our update of the classic carrot-and-raisin salad.

1 **tsp. loosely packed orange zest**	1 **Tbsp. honey**
¼ **cup fresh orange juice**	1 **tsp. Dijon mustard**
2 **Tbsp. chopped dried dates**	½ **tsp. kosher salt**
1 **Tbsp. finely chopped shallot**	½ **cup canola oil**
2 **Tbsp. apple cider vinegar**	

Process orange zest, orange juice, dates, shallot, vinegar, honey, Dijon mustard, and kosher salt in a blender or food processor 30 to 60 seconds or until smooth. With processor running, pour canola oil through food chute in a steady stream, processing until smooth. Makes about 1 cup.

Glazed Turnips and Parsnips

MAKE AHEAD TIP

To make ahead, prepare recipe through Step 1. Then, spread vegetables in a single layer in a jelly-roll pan, and cool. Cover and let stand up to 4 hours. Proceed as directed.

MAKES: 6 TO 8 SERVINGS   HANDS-ON: 50 MIN.   TOTAL: 55 MIN.

2   lb. turnips, peeled and cut into ½-inch-thick wedges
1   lb. parsnips, peeled and cut into ½-inch slices
1½ cups frozen pearl onions
2   tsp. kosher salt
3   Tbsp. cane vinegar, divided*
2   Tbsp. butter
2   Tbsp. olive oil
1   (3-inch) cinnamon stick
1   bay leaf
¼   tsp. dried crushed red pepper
¾   cup cane syrup
½   cup vegetable broth

1. Bring first 4 ingredients, 1 Tbsp. vinegar, and water to cover to a boil in a Dutch oven. Cook, stirring occasionally, 12 to 15 minutes or until vegetables are just tender; drain.
2. Cook butter and next 4 ingredients in a large skillet over medium heat, stirring constantly, 1 minute or until butter melts and spices are fragrant. Add turnip mixture; sauté 8 to 10 minutes or until lightly browned and tender. Discard bay leaf and cinnamon stick.
3. Stir in cane syrup, broth, and remaining 2 Tbsp. vinegar, and cook, stirring often, 8 to 10 minutes or until mixture is slightly thickened and vegetables are coated. Add salt to taste.

* Apple cider may be substituted.

Note: We tested with Steen's Pure Louisiana Cane Vinegar.

Be sure to cut the parsnips and turnips into uniform pieces so that they will cook evenly.

**Asparagus with
Curry Dip**

Asparagus with Curry Dip

*The zesty condiment gives a classic side dish an extra kick with spices
like curry, horseradish, and hot sauce.*

MAKES: 2 ¼ CUPS HANDS-ON: 10 MIN. TOTAL: 10 MIN.

2	cups mayonnaise	2	tsp. grated onion
1	Tbsp. curry powder	1	tsp. celery seeds
2	Tbsp. mustard-mayonnaise sauce	1	tsp. hot sauce
2	Tbsp. ketchup	1	garlic clove, pressed
1	Tbsp. prepared horseradish	3	to 4 lb. steamed fresh asparagus
1	Tbsp. Worcestershire sauce		

Stir together mayonnaise, curry powder, mustard-mayonnaise sauce, ketchup, horseradish, Worcestershire sauce, onion, celery seeds, hot sauce, and garlic. Add salt to taste. Serve with steamed fresh asparagus.

Note: We tested with Hellmann's Real Mayonnaise and Durkee Famous Sauce.

Sweet Potato Spoon Bread

*Cornmeal is a key ingredient in this soufflé-like side from Durham, North Carolina, chef Sara Foster.
It provides structure so the spoon bread won't fall in the center, even after you scoop out a serving.*

MAKES: 8 TO 10 SERVINGS HANDS-ON: 1 HOUR TOTAL: 2 HOURS

2 ½	cups milk	6	Tbsp. butter
1	Tbsp. fresh thyme leaves	3	medium-size sweet potatoes, baked, peeled, and mashed
2	tsp. sea salt		
½	tsp. ground black pepper	5	large eggs, separated
Pinch of ground red pepper		2	tsp. baking powder
1	cup plain yellow cornmeal		

1. Preheat oven to 350°. Bring first 5 ingredients to a simmer in a 3-qt. saucepan over medium heat. Whisk cornmeal into milk mixture in a slow, steady stream. Cook, whisking constantly, 2 to 3 minutes or until mixture thickens and pulls away from bottom of pan. Remove from heat, and stir in butter. Cool 10 minutes.

2. Place potatoes in a large bowl; stir in cornmeal mixture. Stir in egg yolks and baking powder, stirring until well blended.

3. Beat egg whites at high speed with an electric mixer until soft peaks form; fold into potato mixture. Spoon batter into a well-greased (with butter) 3-qt. baking dish.

4. Bake at 350° for 40 to 45 minutes or until golden brown and puffy. (Edges will be firm and center will still be slightly soft.) Cool 10 minutes on a wire rack before serving.

Virginia's Cheesy
Broccoli-and-Rice Casserole

Cheesy Broccoli-and-Rice Casserole

"The old-school version of this recipe uses canned soup and often calls for frozen broccoli. My new twist is made with fresh, wholesome ingredients. It takes just a smidgen more time, but the results are absolutely extraordinary."
—Contributing Editor Virginia Willis, author of Lighten Up, Y'all

MAKES: 8 TO 10 SERVINGS HANDS-ON: 30 MIN. TOTAL: 1 HOUR 5 MIN.

6   Tbsp. unsalted butter, divided
1   cup panko (Japanese breadcrumbs)
2   cups (8 oz.) shredded extra-sharp Cheddar cheese, divided
3   cups reduced-sodium fat-free chicken broth
2   cups milk
1   bay leaf
1   fresh thyme sprig
2   cups chopped onion
½   cup diced celery
1   (8-oz.) package sliced cremini mushrooms

1   tsp. kosher salt, divided
Pinch of freshly ground black pepper
Pinch of ground red pepper
2   garlic cloves, minced
¼   cup all-purpose flour
1½ cups uncooked long-grain rice
½   cup sour cream
½   cup mayonnaise
⅛   tsp. freshly grated nutmeg
3   cups fresh broccoli florets (about 2 heads)

1. Preheat oven to 350°. Melt 2 Tbsp. butter. Combine melted butter with panko and 1 cup shredded Cheddar cheese; toss to coat.

2. Bring broth and next 3 ingredients to a simmer in a medium saucepan over medium-low heat. Reduce heat to low; cover and keep mixture warm until ready to use.

3. Melt remaining 4 Tbsp. butter in a large shallow Dutch oven or ovenproof skillet over medium heat. Add onion and celery to Dutch oven, and cook, stirring occasionally, 3 to 5 minutes or until onion is lightly browned. Add mushrooms to Dutch oven, and stir in ½ tsp. kosher salt and a pinch each of black pepper and ground red pepper. Cook, stirring occasionally, 3 to 5 minutes or until mushrooms are tender. Add garlic, and cook, stirring constantly, 45 seconds. Stir in flour until combined. (Mixture will be dry.)

4. Remove and discard bay leaf and thyme from broth mixture. Gradually stir warm broth mixture into mushroom mixture. Add remaining 1 cup cheese, and stir until well blended and smooth. Stir in rice and next 3 ingredients. Cover Dutch oven with a tight-fitting lid.

5. Bake at 350° for 25 to 30 minutes or until rice is tender and liquid is absorbed. Remove Dutch oven from oven; increase oven temperature to broil.

6. Microwave broccoli, ¼ cup water, and the remaining ½ tsp. kosher salt in a covered microwave-safe bowl at HIGH about 2 minutes or just until broccoli is tender and bright green. Drain and pat broccoli dry. Stir broccoli into rice mixture in Dutch oven. If desired, lightly grease a broiler-safe serving dish with cooking spray; transfer broccoli mixture to serving dish.

7. Sprinkle breadcrumb mixture over broccoli mixture. Place on middle oven rack, and broil 2 to 3 minutes or until topping is golden brown. Let stand 5 minutes before serving.

Buttermilk Mashed Potatoes

Leave the potatoes chunky and rustic, or smash them smooth, depending on what you prefer.

MAKES: 6 SERVINGS HANDS-ON: 25 MIN. TOTAL: 1 HOUR 5 MIN.

2 ½ lb. russet potatoes, peeled and cubed
Parchment paper
1 ½ cups milk

1   cup butter, softened
1 ½ cups buttermilk
Garnishes: chopped fresh chives, butter

1. Preheat oven to 225°. Place potatoes in a large saucepan with water to cover 2 inches. Bring to a boil over medium heat; boil 25 minutes or until potatoes are tender. Drain and spread potatoes in a parchment paper-lined jelly-roll pan. Bake 15 minutes or until potatoes are dry.
2. Bring milk and butter to a simmer in a large saucepan over medium heat, stirring occasionally. (Do not boil.)
3. Transfer potatoes to a large bowl. Add hot milk mixture, and mash potatoes using a potato masher. Gradually add buttermilk, and mash until desired consistency is reached. Add salt and pepper to taste. Garnish, if desired. Serve immediately.

Herbed Couscous

Like a blank canvas, these wonderful fluffy couscous grains pair beautifully with so many flavors. We love the blend of chopped herbs and tangy lemon. Use your favorite herbs to make this versatile side.

MAKES: 6 SERVINGS HANDS-ON: 10 MIN. TOTAL: 20 MIN.

4   cups reduced-sodium chicken broth
2   Tbsp. butter
1   Tbsp. extra virgin olive oil
1 ½ tsp. kosher salt
2   cups uncooked plain couscous
1   Tbsp. chopped fresh flat-leaf parsley

1   Tbsp. chopped fresh chives
1   tsp. chopped fresh rosemary
1   tsp. chopped fresh thyme
1   tsp. loosely packed lemon zest
1   Tbsp. fresh lemon juice

Bring first 4 ingredients to a boil in a medium saucepan over medium-high heat. Stir in couscous; cover and remove pan from heat. Let stand 10 minutes. Uncover and fluff with a fork. Stir in parsley and next 5 ingredients. Add salt and pepper to taste.

Herbed Couscous

Buttermilk
Mashed Potatoes

Mimi's Cornbread Dressing

MAKES: **8 TO 10 SERVINGS** HANDS-ON: **30 MIN.** TOTAL: **2 HOURS 5 MIN.**

2	Tbsp. canola oil, divided	2	cups chopped celery
2	cups self-rising white cornmeal mix	4	large eggs, lightly beaten
1⅓	cups buttermilk	⅔	cup chopped fresh flat-leaf parsley
1	cup self-rising flour	1	Tbsp. chopped fresh sage
2	large eggs, lightly beaten	2	tsp. chopped fresh thyme
5	to 6 cups reduced-sodium chicken broth	1½	tsp. freshly ground black pepper
¾	cup butter, divided	½	tsp. kosher salt
3	cups chopped sweet onion (1 large)		

1. Preheat oven to 400°. Coat bottom and sides of a 10-inch cast-iron skillet with 1 Tbsp. oil; heat in oven 10 minutes.

2. Meanwhile, stir together cornmeal mix, next 3 ingredients, and remaining 1 Tbsp. oil. Pour batter into hot skillet.

3. Bake at 400° for 30 minutes or until golden. Remove to a wire rack; cool 15 minutes. Crumble cornbread into a large bowl. Stir 5 cups broth into crumbled cornbread until moistened, adding more broth, 1 Tbsp. at a time, if necessary. (Mixture should resemble wet sand.)

4. Melt ¼ cup butter in a large skillet over medium-high heat; add onion and celery, and sauté 8 to 10 minutes or until tender. Add onion mixture to cornbread mixture.

5. Lightly grease a 13- x 9-inch baking dish with cooking spray. Microwave remaining ½ cup butter in a small microwave-safe bowl at HIGH 1 minute or until melted. Stir melted butter, eggs, and remaining ingredients into cornbread mixture; spoon into baking dish.

6. Bake at 400° for 50 minutes to 1 hour or until golden brown. Serve immediately.

Packaged mixes and store-bought cornbread vary in sweetness and moisture, so for this savory dressing, make yours from scratch. This simple buttermilk skillet version will give your dressing the best texture and flavor.

Smoked Oyster-and-Andouille Dressing

Give your dressing an extra-savory depth of flavor with the addition of humble canned, smoked oysters.

MAKES: **8 TO 10 SERVINGS** HANDS-ON: **1 HOUR** TOTAL: **2 HOURS 10 MIN.**

5	cups crumbled cornbread	2	Tbsp. chopped fresh thyme
8	oz. sourdough bread slices, cut into ½-inch cubes (5 cups)	2	Tbsp. chopped fresh rosemary
1	cup butter	1	Tbsp. Cajun blackened seasoning
2	cups diced andouille sausage	1	Tbsp. poultry seasoning
2	cups chopped onion (about 1 large)	1	tsp. black pepper
2	cups finely chopped celery (4 to 5 ribs)	3	(3.75-oz.) cans smoked oysters, drained
1	cup chopped green bell pepper	4	cups chicken broth
¼	cup chopped fresh sage	4	large eggs, lightly beaten
			Garnish: chopped fresh rosemary

1. Preheat oven to 400°. Stir together cornbread and bread cubes in a large bowl. Melt butter in a large saucepan over medium heat. Add sausage, and cook, covered and stirring occasionally, 5 to 7 minutes or until butter turns a light orange. Remove sausage with a slotted spoon; drain on paper towels.

2. Add onion and next 2 ingredients to butter; sauté 8 minutes or until tender. Add sage and next 2 ingredients, and sauté 1 minute. Stir in Cajun seasoning and next 2 ingredients; remove from heat.

3. Stir vegetables and sausage into cornbread mixture. Stir in oysters and next 2 ingredients. Lightly grease a 13- x 9-inch baking dish with cooking spray. Spread cornbread mixture in baking dish; cover with aluminum foil.

4. Bake, covered, at 400° for 30 minutes. Uncover and bake 30 more minutes or until browned and thoroughly cooked. Let stand 10 minutes before serving. Garnish, if desired.

Note: We tested with Weber N'Orleans Cajun Seasoning and cornbread made with Martha White Cotton Country Cornbread Mix. (Do not use a sweet cornbread mix, such as Jiffy.)

Old-School Cranberry Salad

"My cranberry salad has become a staple at our Thanksgiving table because of its beautiful color, taste, and texture. Everyone seems to love this dish. I started adding the maraschino cherries to temper the tartness of the cranberries. The other fruits were added to satisfy family members' tastes. This recipe has a lot of flexibility, and that's why I love it so much."
—SL reader Shawn Jackson, Fishers, IN

MAKES: 8 TO 10 SERVINGS   HANDS-ON: 20 MIN.   TOTAL: 2 HOURS 55 MIN.

4 cups fresh cranberries	1 cup peeled and chopped Bartlett pears (about 2 pears)
¾ cup sugar	½ cup drained mandarin oranges
½ cup fresh orange juice	½ cup drained pineapple tidbits
1 cup drained maraschino cherries	

Bring first 3 ingredients and ½ cup water to a boil in a large saucepan over medium-high heat, stirring often. Reduce heat to medium, and simmer, stirring occasionally, 20 to 25 minutes or until cranberries pop and mixture thickens. Remove from heat, and let stand 15 minutes. Stir in cherries and remaining ingredients. Transfer to a bowl; cover and chill 2 to 12 hours.

New-School Cranberry Salad

We were so inspired by Old-School Cranberry Salad that we created a new version using fresh oranges and pineapple in place of canned and subbing dried cherries for maraschinos.

MAKES: 8 TO 10 SERVINGS   HANDS-ON: 25 MIN.   TOTAL: 3 HOURS

4 cups fresh cranberries	1 cup peeled and chopped Bartlett pears (about 2 pears)
1 cup dried cherries	½ cup chopped fresh pineapple
¾ cup sugar	Garnishes: orange slices, fresh rosemary sprigs
½ cup fresh orange juice	
1 cup orange segments	

Bring first 4 ingredients and ¼ cup water to a boil in a large saucepan over medium-high heat, stirring often. Reduce heat to medium, and simmer, stirring occasionally, 20 to 25 minutes or until cranberries pop and mixture thickens. Remove from heat, and let stand 15 minutes. Stir in orange segments and remaining ingredients. Transfer to a bowl; cover and chill 2 to 12 hours. Garnish, if desired.

ENTRÉES FOR EVERY OCCASION

*Build your meal around one of these
festive and hearty main dishes*

Smoked Self-Basting Turkey

Chris Lilly, one of our favorite pitmasters and four-time Memphis in May grand champion, taught SL recipe tester and developer Pam Lolley this cool technique. The key? Mounding herb butter on top of the breast, covering the bird with aluminum foil, and cutting a slit in the foil. The butter will slowly melt and baste the turkey as it cooks, and the smoke will permeate the bird through the hole. Find more techniques in Chris' book, Fire & Smoke.

MAKES: 8 TO 10 SERVINGS   HANDS-ON: 20 MIN.   TOTAL: 6 HOURS 50 MIN.

1   (12- to 14-lb.) whole fresh or frozen turkey, thawed
2   Tbsp. kosher salt
2   tsp. freshly ground black pepper
2   fresh thyme sprigs
2   fresh sage sprigs
Kitchen string

1   (12 ⅞- x 10-inch) disposable aluminum foil roasting pan
1   cup butter, softened
2   tsp. chopped fresh sage
1   tsp. chopped fresh thyme
1   to 2 cups hickory or oak wood chips

1. Light 1 side of grill, heating to 225° to 250°; leave other side unlit. Close grill lid, and maintain temperature 15 to 20 minutes.

2. Remove giblets and neck from turkey; pat turkey dry. Sprinkle salt and pepper over skin and inside turkey cavity; place thyme sprigs and sage sprigs inside cavity. Tie ends of legs together with string, and tuck wing tips under; place turkey, breast side up, in pan.

3. Stir together softened butter, chopped sage, and chopped thyme. Shape butter mixture into a 2-inch ball; press ball firmly onto top of turkey breast. Cover roasting pan with a double layer of heavy-duty aluminum foil, sealing edges tightly. Cut a 2- x 1-inch hole in foil directly over butter.

4. Place wood chips directly on hot coals. Place pan with turkey on unlit side of grill; cover with grill lid.

5. Smoke turkey, maintaining temperature inside grill between 225° and 250°, for 6 to 7 hours or until a meat thermometer inserted in thickest portion of turkey thigh registers 165° to 170°. Peel back foil from turkey during last 1 to 1 ½ hours of cooking time.

6. Remove turkey from grill; let stand 15 minutes before carving.

Dry Brined-Herb Roasted Turkey

Skip the cumbersome wet brines that call for soaking turkey and making the skin flabby. This classic overnight dry brine—a simple herb, salt, and sugar mixture—gives the turkey deep flavor and a crackly crust. Be adventurous and create your own signature dry brine using our sugar and salt ratios as a guide, or try one of our three variations below.

MAKES: 8 TO 10 SERVINGS HANDS-ON: 25 MIN. TOTAL: 13 HOURS 25 MIN.

3 Tbsp. kosher salt	1 (12- to 14-lb.) whole fresh or frozen turkey, thawed
3 Tbsp. dark brown sugar	½ cup butter, softened
2 tsp. rubbed sage	Wooden picks
2 tsp. dried thyme	Kitchen string
1½ tsp. freshly ground black pepper	
1 tsp. garlic powder	

1. Stir together first 6 ingredients.
2. Remove giblets and neck from turkey; pat turkey dry. Sprinkle 1 Tbsp. brine into cavity; rub into cavity. Reserve 1 Tbsp. brine, and sprinkle outside of turkey with remaining brine; rub into skin. Chill turkey 10 to 24 hours.
3. Preheat oven to 350°. Stir together butter and reserved 1 Tbsp. brine. Loosen skin from turkey breast without totally detaching skin; spread butter mixture under skin. Replace skin, securing with wooden picks.
4. Tie ends of legs together with string; tuck wing tips under. Lightly grease a wire rack with cooking spray, and place rack in a large roasting pan. Place turkey, breast side up, on rack in pan.
5. Bake at 350° for 2 hours and 30 minutes or until a meat thermometer inserted in thickest portion of turkey thigh registers 165°. Remove from oven; let stand 30 minutes before carving.

Cajun-Brine Roasted Turkey: Prepare recipe as directed, substituting paprika for sage, dried oregano for dried thyme, and 2 tsp. ground red pepper for black pepper.

Jerk-Brine Roasted Turkey: Prepare recipe as directed, substituting allspice for sage and onion powder for garlic powder and adding 2 tsp. ground cumin to brine mixture.

Five Spice-Brine Roasted Turkey: Prepare recipe as directed, substituting Chinese five spice for sage and ground ginger for thyme.

Nashville Hot Turkey

For you serious spice hounds, try this ode to the city's incendiary fried chicken.
Use black pepper bacon or any bacon to flavor the peanut oil.

MAKES: 8 TO 10 SERVINGS HANDS-ON: 25 MIN. TOTAL: 2 HOURS 20 MIN.

Peanut oil (about 3 gal.)
1   (12- to 14-lb.) whole fresh or frozen turkey, thawed
2   Tbsp. kosher salt
2   tsp. freshly ground black pepper

1   (1-lb.) package thick pepper bacon slices
¼   cup ground red pepper
1   Tbsp. dark brown sugar
1   tsp. paprika
½   tsp. garlic powder

1. Pour oil into a deep propane turkey fryer 10 to 12 inches from top; heat to 350° over a medium-low flame according to manufacturer's instructions (about 45 minutes).

2. Meanwhile, remove giblets and neck from turkey; pat turkey dry. Stir together salt and pepper. Sprinkle 1 Tbsp. salt mixture inside cavity; rub into cavity. Sprinkle outside of turkey with remaining salt mixture; rub into skin. Let turkey stand at room temperature 30 minutes.

3. Using long-handled tongs, carefully lower bacon, 1 slice at a time, into hot oil. Fry 1 to 2 minutes or until bacon is brown and crisp. Drain bacon on a paper towel-lined baking sheet; reserve bacon for another use.

4. Place turkey on fryer rod. Carefully lower turkey into hot oil with rod attachment. Fry 35 to 45 minutes or until a meat thermometer inserted in thickest portion of turkey thigh registers 165° (about 3 minutes per pound plus an additional 5 minutes). Keep oil temperature between 325° and 345°. Remove turkey from oil; drain and let stand 30 minutes before carving. Reserve 1 cup frying oil from fryer.

5. Stir together ground red pepper, brown sugar, paprika, and garlic powder in a medium saucepan. Carefully whisk in reserved 1 cup frying oil, and cook over low heat, stirring constantly, 5 minutes. Brush mixture over turkey, and serve immediately.

Note: We tested with LouAna Peanut Oil.

Grill-Smoked Turkey

MAKES: 8 SERVINGS   HANDS-ON: 30 MIN.   TOTAL: 17 HOURS 45 MIN., INCLUDING BRINE

1   (10- to 12-lb.) fresh or frozen turkey, thawed
Herb-Salt Dry Brine (recipe below)
4   cups applewood chips
3   carrots, halved
1   apple, halved
1   small onion, halved

Kitchen string
2   (12 ⅞- x 10-inch) disposable aluminum foil
    roasting pans
3   Tbsp. canola oil
Freshly ground black pepper

1. Remove giblets and neck from turkey; pat turkey dry. Rub ¼ cup Herb-Salt Dry Brine into cavity. Rub skin with remaining brine. Cover and chill 14 to 24 hours.
2. Soak wood chips 30 minutes.
3. Meanwhile, rinse turkey; drain cavity well, and pat dry. Place carrots and next 2 ingredients in cavity. Tie ends of legs together with kitchen string; tuck wing tips under.
4. Light 1 side of grill, heating to 300° to 325° (medium-low) heat, leaving other side unlit. Close grill lid, and maintain internal temperature at 300° to 325°.
5. Drain wood chips, and place in center of a 12- x 20-inch piece of heavy-duty aluminum foil. Wrap to form a packet. Pierce several holes in packet; place directly on lit side of grill.
6. Place 1 disposable roasting pan inside second pan. Place turkey, breast side up, in pan, and brush turkey with oil. Sprinkle with desired amount of pepper.
7. Smoke turkey, covered with grill lid and maintaining internal temperature at 300° to 325°, 2 hours and 45 minutes to 3 hours and 15 minutes or until a meat thermometer inserted in thickest portion registers 165°. Remove carrots, onion, and apple from cavity, and discard. Let turkey stand 30 minutes at room temperature before slicing.

Herb-Salt Dry Brine

⅓   cup kosher salt
⅓   cup sugar
2   Tbsp. chopped fresh rosemary

2   Tbsp. chopped fresh thyme
2   Tbsp. chopped fresh sage

Stir together all ingredients. Makes about 1 cup.

Turkey Roulade with Figgy Port Wine Sauce

Thick slices of bacon and spinach are rolled into turkey breasts and baked to perfection for this impressive main dish. A fruity port sauce completes this holiday dish.

MAKES: 6 TO 8 SERVINGS HANDS-ON: 1 HOUR 10 MIN. TOTAL: 1 HOUR 45 MIN.

8	thick bacon slices, chopped	½	cup finely chopped dried golden figs
2	shallots, minced	1	cup port wine
4	garlic cloves, minced	3	Tbsp. olive oil
¼	tsp. dried crushed red pepper	½	cup red wine vinegar
2	(20-oz.) packages fresh baby spinach	1	cup chicken broth
1	(6- to 7-lb.) bone-in turkey breast	2	Tbsp. plum jam
6	(6-inch) fresh rosemary sprigs	1	Tbsp. cold butter
Kitchen string		**Garnish: fresh rosemary sprigs**	

1. Cook bacon in a Dutch oven over medium heat 10 to 15 minutes or until crisp. Remove bacon, and drain on paper towels, reserving 3 Tbsp. drippings in Dutch oven. Sauté shallots and next 2 ingredients in hot drippings 1 to 2 minutes or until tender. Add spinach, in batches, and sauté 5 minutes or until wilted. Drain mixture, and coarsely chop. Stir together bacon and spinach mixture in a large bowl; add salt and pepper to taste. Cool 10 minutes.

2. Remove bone from turkey. Butterfly turkey breasts by making a lengthwise cut in 1 side, cutting to but not through the opposite side; unfold. Place breasts between 2 sheets of heavy-duty plastic wrap, and flatten to ¼-inch thickness, using a rolling pin or the flat side of a meat mallet. Sprinkle both sides with desired amount of salt and pepper, and place, skin sides down, on work surface.

3. Spoon half of spinach mixture on 1 breast, leaving a ½-inch border. Roll up, jelly-roll fashion, starting with long skinless side. Place 3 rosemary sprigs on breast, and tie with kitchen string, securing at 2-inch intervals. Repeat procedure with remaining breast, spinach mixture, and rosemary sprigs.

4. Preheat oven to 425°. Bring figs and port to a boil in a medium saucepan over high heat. Reduce heat to medium-low; simmer, stirring occasionally, 5 minutes or until figs are tender. Remove from heat.

5. Cook turkey in hot olive oil in a 12- to 13-inch nonstick ovenproof skillet over medium-high heat 2 minutes on each side or until browned. If necessary, turn turkey so that rosemary sides are up. Transfer skillet to oven, and bake at 425° for 25 to 30 minutes or until a meat thermometer inserted into thickest portion registers 165°.

6. Transfer turkey to a wire rack. Discard fat in skillet. Add fig mixture and vinegar to skillet, and cook over medium-high heat, stirring constantly, 4 to 5 minutes or until thickened. Stir in broth, and simmer, stirring occasionally, 5 to 8 minutes or until reduced by half. Stir in plum jam, and cook, stirring constantly, 1 minute. Whisk in butter; add salt and pepper to taste.

7. Remove and discard kitchen string from turkey. Cut turkey into ½-inch-thick slices, and serve with fig mixture.

Lemon-Rosemary-Garlic Chicken and Potatoes

MAKES: 6 SERVINGS HANDS-ON: 20 MIN. TOTAL: 1 HOUR 5 MIN.

⅓ cup olive oil
¼ cup fresh lemon juice
1 (3.5-oz.) jar capers, drained
2 lemons, sliced
10 garlic cloves, smashed
3 Tbsp. fresh rosemary leaves
2 tsp. kosher salt

1 tsp. freshly ground black pepper
3 Tbsp. olive oil
6 chicken legs (about 1 ½ lb.)
4 skin-on, bone-in chicken thighs (about 2 ½ lb.)
2 lb. small red potatoes
Crusty French bread

1. Preheat oven to 450°. Stir together first 8 ingredients in a medium bowl.
2. Place a roasting pan on stovetop over 2 burners. Add 3 Tbsp. olive oil, and heat over medium-high heat. Sprinkle chicken with desired amount of salt and pepper; place, skin sides down, in pan. Add potatoes. Cook 9 to 10 minutes or until chicken is browned. Turn chicken, and pour lemon mixture over chicken.
3. Bake at 450° for 45 to 50 minutes or until chicken is done. Serve chicken with sauce and French bread.

Roast Chicken

MAKES: 4 TO 6 SERVINGS HANDS-ON TIME: 20 MIN. TOTAL TIME: 1 HOUR 35 MIN.

1 (4- to 5-lb.) whole chicken
1 ½ tsp. kosher salt, divided
1 lemon half
1 tsp. seasoned pepper

1 tsp. dried rosemary
1 Tbsp. olive oil
1 Tbsp. butter, melted

1. Preheat oven to 450°. If applicable, remove neck and giblets from chicken, and reserve for another use. Rinse chicken with cold water, and drain cavity well. Pat dry with paper towels. Sprinkle ½ tsp. salt inside cavity. Place lemon half inside cavity.
2. Lightly grease a wire rack and a shallow roasting pan with cooking spray. Stir together pepper, rosemary, and remaining 1 tsp. salt. Brush outside of chicken with oil. Rub 2 ½ tsp. pepper mixture into skin. Sprinkle remaining pepper mixture over both sides of breast. Place chicken, breast side up, on rack in pan. Add ¾ cup water to pan.
3. Bake at 450° for 20 minutes. Reduce heat to 375°, and bake 30 minutes. Baste chicken with pan juices; drizzle with melted butter. Bake 15 to 25 minutes or until a meat thermometer inserted in thigh registers 165°, shielding with aluminum foil to prevent excessive browning, if necessary. Remove chicken from oven, and baste with pan juices. Let stand 10 minutes before slicing.

Note: We tested with McCormick Gourmet Collection Crushed Rosemary.

Lemon-Rosemary-
Garlic Chicken and
Potatoes

Molasses-Brined Roasted Chicken

MAKES: **8 SERVINGS** HANDS-ON: **45 MIN.** TOTAL: **8 HOURS 25 MIN.**

½ cup kosher salt
½ cup dark molasses
2 cups ice cubes
1 sweet onion, thinly sliced
2 fresh thyme sprigs
2 garlic cloves, peeled and sliced
½ tsp. black peppercorns

2 (4- to 5-lb.) whole chickens, cut into 4 pieces each (boneless breasts with first wing joint intact, legs whole with bone in, carcasses reserved)*
½ tsp. garlic salt
2 Tbsp. canola oil
8 garlic cloves, unpeeled
2 fresh thyme sprigs
Garnish: fresh thyme sprigs

1. Bring 4 cups water to a boil in a large Dutch oven over medium-high heat. Add kosher salt and molasses. Reduce heat to low, and simmer, stirring occasionally, 2 to 3 minutes or until salt and molasses dissolve. Transfer to a very large bowl; add ice and next 4 ingredients. Let stand, stirring occasionally, 30 minutes or until mixture cools to room temperature. Cover and chill 30 minutes to 1 hour or until cold.
2. Submerge chicken in cold brine. Cover and chill 6 to 8 hours.
3. Preheat oven to 400°. Remove chicken from brine; rinse and pat dry. Sprinkle with garlic salt.
4. Heat 1 Tbsp. oil in a 14-inch nonstick or cast-iron skillet over medium-high heat. Add 4 unpeeled garlic cloves, 1 thyme sprig, and half of chicken. Cook 5 minutes or until skin is browned and crisp. (The molasses in the brine will brown the skin quickly.) Turn chicken and garlic, and cook 5 minutes or until browned. Remove chicken, and place on a wire rack in a jelly-roll pan. Wipe skillet clean. Repeat with remaining oil, chicken, garlic, and thyme.
5. Bake chicken, skin side up, at 400° for 10 to 20 minutes or until a meat thermometer inserted into thickest portion registers 165°. (Breasts will cook faster than legs, so check for doneness after 10 minutes.) Cover with aluminum foil. Let stand 10 minutes before serving. Garnish, if desired.

* 8 chicken leg quarters or 8 chicken breasts, airline cut, may be substituted.

Note: We tested with Diamond Crystal Kosher Salt.

Prosciutto-Wrapped Duck with Gumbo Gravy

Use paper-thin sliced prosciutto to wrap the duck, and sub chicken thighs for wild duck, if needed.

MAKES: 6 TO 8 SERVINGS HANDS-ON: 20 MIN. TOTAL: 9 HOURS 50 MIN., INCLUDING GRAVY

2	cups buttermilk	½	tsp. Cajun seasoning
2	Tbsp. hot sauce	8	thin prosciutto slices
1½	tsp. kosher salt	2	Tbsp. vegetable oil
8	wild duck breasts or skinned and boned chicken thighs		Rice
			Gumbo Gravy (recipe below)

1. Combine first 3 ingredients in a zip-top plastic bag; add duck and seal. Chill 8 hours.

2. Preheat oven to 400°. Remove duck; discard marinade. Pat duck dry; sprinkle with Cajun seasoning. Wrap each duck breast with 1 prosciutto slice.

3. Brown duck in hot oil in a skillet over medium-high heat 2 minutes on each side. Place duck on a wire rack in a jelly-roll pan.

4. Bake at 400° for 6 minutes (10 minutes for chicken) or until a meat thermometer registers 145° or to desired degree of doneness (165° for chicken). Let stand 10 minutes. Serve with rice and gravy.

Gumbo Gravy

1	lb. andouille sausage	3	bay leaves
6	Tbsp. canola oil, divided	2	celery ribs, diced
8	oz. button mushrooms, stemmed and quartered	2	garlic cloves, minced
2	Tbsp. brandy or bourbon	1	green bell pepper, diced
¼	cup all-purpose flour	5	green onions, sliced
½	tsp. Cajun seasoning	2	cups reduced-sodium chicken broth
¼	tsp. dried thyme		Hot sauce
		⅛	tsp. gumbo filé powder (optional)

1. Slice sausage; cook in 1 Tbsp. hot oil in a Dutch oven over medium-high heat 5 minutes. Remove sausage; drain. Reserve drippings in skillet. Add 1 Tbsp. oil; reduce heat to medium. Cook mushrooms 5 minutes or until brown. Add to sausage.

2. Remove skillet from heat; add brandy. Return skillet to heat; cook 1 minute. Stir in flour and remaining 4 Tbsp. oil; cook, stirring to loosen browned bits, 8 minutes or until roux is the color of chocolate.

3. Stir in Cajun seasoning, next 5 ingredients, and white parts of green onions; cook, stirring constantly, 7 minutes. Add broth; cook, stirring constantly, 5 minutes. Return sausage and mushrooms to pan; cook 20 minutes. Add hot sauce to taste. Discard bay leaves. Sprinkle with gumbo filé powder, if desired. Top with green parts of green onions. Makes 8 servings.

Ham Glazed with Spiced Plum Conserve

Any brined, smoked supermarket ham will be welcomed on your holiday table in addition to (or in lieu of) the turkey. If you're using a spiral ham, there's no need to score it and stud with cloves.

MAKES: 8 TO 10 SERVINGS HANDS-ON: 15 MIN. TOTAL: 5 HOURS 45 MIN., INCLUDING CONSERVE

1 (8-lb.) fully cooked, bone-in ham	3 cups Spiced Plum Conserve (recipe below)
1 Tbsp. whole cloves	

Preheat oven to 325°. Place ham in an aluminum foil-lined 13- x 9-inch pan. Make shallow cuts in fat 1 inch apart in a diamond pattern. Insert cloves in centers of diamonds. Pour conserve over ham, add ½ cup water to pan, and cover with foil. Bake 4 hours or until a meat thermometer inserted into thickest portion registers 165°, basting with pan juices every hour. Remove from oven, and let stand 15 minutes before serving.

Spiced Plum Conserve

Experiment with your favorite seasonal fruit, including muscadines. This conserve also pairs well with roasted or smoked pork shoulder.

6 lb. red plums, quartered	3 (3-inch) cinnamon sticks
½ cup apple cider vinegar	3 cups sugar
¼ cup whole cloves	

1. Bring first 4 ingredients to a boil in a Dutch oven over medium-high heat, stirring occasionally; reduce heat to low, and simmer, stirring occasionally, 20 minutes or until mixture thickens. Pour through a fine wire-mesh strainer into a large bowl, discarding solids. Clean Dutch oven. Return plum mixture to Dutch oven.

2. Bring to a boil over medium heat; add sugar, and simmer, stirring often, 10 minutes or until slightly thickened. Let stand 15 minutes. Use immediately, or refrigerate in an airtight container up to 3 weeks. Makes about 6 cups.

Cracklin'-Fresh Picnic Ham with Apple-Cranberry-Pomegranate Salsa

Ask your butcher: While a holiday ham traditionally consists of a cured, brined, or smoked cut of pork from the hind leg, we're taking liberties with the word "ham" and choosing the best cut for this job—the shoulder. Order a skin-on fresh picnic ham, aka the picnic cut, a forgiving, economical joint that will give you the juiciest results.

MAKES: 8 TO 10 SERVINGS HANDS-ON: 30 MIN.
TOTAL: 14 HOURS 20 MIN., INCLUDING SALSA, PLUS 2 DAYS FOR CHILLING

1 (11 ⅔-lb.) bone-in, skin-on fresh pork picnic shoulder (picnic ham)	½ cup kosher salt
Clean box cutter or one-sided razor blade	2 tsp. freshly ground black pepper
	Apple-Cranberry-Pomegranate Salsa (recipe below)

First, plan ahead. A bone-in roast this thick requires two days of seasoning to allow the salt to penetrate to the bone. (That's as many days as ingredients required to flavor this budget-minded wonder.) Second, score the skin using a box cutter or razor blade so the fat renders as it cooks and the exterior turns potato chip crunchy.

The right temp: Because we're talking shoulder, go for an internal temp of at least 175°, which will encourage the connective tissue to break down and intramuscular fat to melt.

1. Make ¼-inch-deep cuts ¼ inch apart in skin of ham with a clean box cutter. (The sharp blades cut through the skin with ease and make straight edges.) Stir together salt and pepper; rub over ham, working into cuts in skin. Place ham in a very large bowl, and cover with plastic wrap. Chill 2 days.
2. Remove ham from bowl. Brush salt from ham, and discard. Place ham, fat side up, on a wire rack in a jelly-roll pan, and chill, uncovered, 8 to 10 hours to air-dry.
3. Let ham stand at room temperature 1 hour.
4. Preheat oven to 425°. Bake ham on lower oven rack 45 minutes. Reduce oven temperature to 325°, and bake 2 hours and 30 minutes. Increase oven temperature to 425°, and bake 30 to 35 minutes or until skin is crisp and a meat thermometer inserted into the thickest portion registers 175°. Let stand 30 minutes before slicing. Serve with salsa.

Apple-Cranberry-Pomegranate Salsa

This bracing and fresh all-purpose condiment pairs well with any holiday pork roast or turkey. Look for refrigerated prepackaged pomegranate seeds in the supermarket, or buy whole fruit for the recipe and garnish with any extra.

¼ cup sugar	¼ cup pomegranate seeds
¼ cup dry white wine	¼ cup coarsely chopped toasted walnuts
¼ cup water	1 Tbsp. loosely packed orange zest
¼ cup halved sweetened dried cranberries	1 Tbsp. chopped fresh flat-leaf parsley
1 large Granny Smith apple, diced	2 Tbsp. extra virgin olive oil
2 Tbsp. fresh lime juice	

Bring sugar, wine, and water to a boil in a small saucepan over medium heat. Remove from heat; add cranberries. Let stand 20 minutes, and drain. Transfer to a bowl. Toss together diced apple and lime juice, and stir into cranberries. Stir in pomegranate seeds, walnuts, orange zest, and parsley. Gradually stir in olive oil. Makes 2 cups.

Herb-Roasted Pork Loin

MAKES: 6 TO 8 SERVINGS HANDS-ON: 25 MIN. TOTAL: 9 HOURS 45 MIN.

2	Tbsp. chopped fresh thyme	2	tsp. freshly ground black pepper
2	Tbsp. chopped fresh rosemary	1	tsp. finely crushed coriander seeds
2	Tbsp. kosher salt	1	tsp. dry mustard
1	Tbsp. loosely packed lemon zest	¼	tsp. dried crushed red pepper
1	Tbsp. light brown sugar	1	(2 ½- to 3-lb.) boneless pork loin
3	garlic cloves, pressed	3	Tbsp. olive oil

1. Combine first 10 ingredients in a small bowl. Rub over pork. Chill, uncovered, 8 to 12 hours.

2. Let pork stand at room temperature 30 minutes. (Bringing it to room temperature will help it cook faster and more evenly.)

3. Preheat oven to 400°. Cook pork in hot oil in a large skillet over medium-high heat 2 minutes on each side or until browned. Lightly grease a wire rack with cooking spray. Place pork on rack in a roasting pan.

4. Bake at 400° for 35 to 45 minutes or until a meat thermometer inserted into thickest portion registers 135°. Remove from oven, and let stand 15 minutes before serving.

Seasoning and chilling the meat uncovered will help form a crust, encouraging a beautiful deep, golden-brown color while cooking.

Sage-Crusted Pork Racks with Pear Chutney

*These mouthwatering pork racks topped with a spiced chutney are
the perfect main dish for your holiday dinner. Have your butcher
French the bones of your pork loin roasts for a more elegant presentation.*

**MAKES: 8 TO 10 SERVINGS HANDS-ON: 1 HOUR 5 MIN.
TOTAL: 13 HOURS 55 MIN., INCLUDING CHUTNEY**

3   cups firmly packed fresh sage leaves
     (about 4 [1-oz.] packages)
3   garlic cloves
7   tsp. kosher salt, divided
1¼ cups olive or canola oil

2   Tbsp. loosely packed orange zest
1½ tsp. dried crushed red pepper
2   (3½- to 4-lb.) 6-rib bone-in pork loin roasts,
     chine bones removed
Pear Chutney (recipe below)

1. Process sage, garlic, and 1 tsp. salt in a food processor 30 to 45 seconds or until finely chopped. Add oil and next 2 ingredients; process 10 to 15 seconds or until blended. Rub mixture over roasts. Cover and chill 10 to 12 hours.

2. Let roasts stand at room temperature 30 minutes. Preheat oven to 500°. Lightly grease a wire rack with cooking spray, and place rack in a roasting pan. Place roasts on rack in pan. Sprinkle remaining 6 tsp. salt over roasts.

3. Bake at 500° for 30 minutes; reduce oven temperature to 325°, and bake 1 hour and 15 minutes or until a meat thermometer inserted into thickest portions registers 155°. Let roasts stand 30 minutes before serving with chutney.

Pear Chutney

This spiced chutney is a sweet complement to savory roasted pork or chicken.

5   ripe pears, peeled and diced
4   Tbsp. olive oil
1   large red onion, cut into ½-inch slices
⅓   cup golden raisins
3   garlic cloves, minced
1   tsp. grated fresh ginger
1   Tbsp. sugar

1   tsp. ground cinnamon
½   tsp. ground cloves
¼   tsp. dried crushed red pepper
⅓   cup red wine vinegar
⅓   cup maple syrup
¼   cup fresh flat-leaf parsley

Cook pears in 2 Tbsp. hot olive oil in a Dutch oven over medium heat, stirring occasionally, 15 to 20 minutes or until tender. Transfer to a bowl; wipe Dutch oven clean. Heat 2 Tbsp. olive oil in Dutch oven over medium heat. Add onion; sauté 8 to 10 minutes or until tender. Add raisins, garlic, and ginger; sauté 5 minutes. Add sugar, cinnamon, cloves, and dried crushed red pepper, and cook, stirring constantly, 1 minute or until spices are fragrant. Stir in vinegar and maple syrup, and cook 3 to 5 minutes or until reduced by half. Stir in pears; cook, stirring constantly, 5 minutes. Stir in parsley. Add salt and pepper to taste. Makes 4 cups.

Standing Rib Roast with Red Wine Mushrooms

Ask your butcher to remove the chine bone. A thin bone that runs perpendicular to the rib bones, it will get in the way of slicing once the meat is roasted and has rested.

MAKES: 8 TO 10 SERVINGS HANDS-ON: 30 MIN. TOTAL: 3 HOURS 55 MIN.

ROAST
- 1 (7-lb.) 4-bone prime rib roast, chine bone removed
- ⅓ cup Dijon mustard
- 3 garlic cloves, minced
- 1 Tbsp. chopped fresh rosemary
- 2 Tbsp. olive oil
- 7 tsp. kosher salt
- 2¼ tsp. freshly ground black pepper

RED WINE MUSHROOMS
- 2 Tbsp. butter
- 2 (8-oz.) packages fresh mushrooms, quartered
- 2 shallots, minced
- ½ cup dry red wine
- 1 cup beef broth

1. Prepare Roast: Let roast stand at room temperature 1 hour.

2. Preheat oven to 450°. Lightly grease a wire rack with cooking spray, and place rack in a roasting pan. Whisk together mustard and next 3 ingredients; reserve 1 Tbsp. mixture. Rub remaining mixture over roast; sprinkle with salt and pepper. Place roast on rack in pan.

3. Bake at 450° on lower oven rack 45 minutes. Reduce oven temperature to 350°; bake 1 hour and 10 minutes or until a meat thermometer inserted into thickest portion registers 120° to 130° (medium-rare) or 130° to 135° (medium). Let stand 30 minutes; transfer roast to a serving platter, reserving drippings in pan.

4. Meanwhile, prepare Red Wine Mushrooms: Skim fat from reserved drippings; place pan on stovetop over 2 burners. Melt butter in pan over medium-high heat, stirring occasionally and moving pan as necessary to prevent hot spots. Add mushrooms; sauté 3 minutes. Add shallots; cook, stirring constantly, 3 to 4 minutes or until tender. Stir in wine; cook, stirring constantly, 2 minutes. Stir in broth; reduce heat to medium, and simmer, stirring constantly, 5 minutes. Stir in reserved 1 Tbsp. mustard mixture. Add salt and pepper to taste. Slice roast, and serve with mushroom mixture.

Note: Start roasting at 450° for 45 minutes to form the caramelized crust. Then reduce the temperature and finish cooking to keep the inside pink and juicy. The right temperature: 125° for prime rib lovers. Remember: The internal temperature on large roasts like this will continue to rise as the roast rests.

Classic Red Wine-Braised Beef Short Ribs

Beef short ribs were made to be braised. As they simmer, the meat becomes tender and pulls away from the bone, adding drama to the plated dish with so little effort. Four pounds of short ribs should give you about 10 good-size, meaty ribs.

MAKES: 6 TO 8 SERVINGS HANDS-ON: 1 HOUR 10 MIN. TOTAL: 17 HOURS 40 MIN.

4 lb. beef short ribs, trimmed	2 medium-size carrots, chopped
1 Tbsp. kosher salt	1 medium-size yellow onion, chopped
1½ tsp. freshly ground black pepper	1 small garlic bulb, cut in half crosswise
4 cups unsalted beef stock	1 bay leaf
¼ cup olive oil	3 fresh flat-leaf parsley sprigs
1¾ cups red wine	3 fresh thyme sprigs
¼ cup brandy or sherry	2 fresh rosemary sprigs
1 cup drained canned whole tomatoes, chopped	Parchment paper
3 celery ribs, chopped	2 Tbsp. butter

1. Sprinkle ribs on all sides with salt and pepper; cover and chill 12 to 24 hours.

2. Preheat oven to 300°. Let ribs stand at room temperature 30 minutes. Bring stock to a boil in a medium saucepan over high heat. Reduce heat to medium and simmer 8 to 10 minutes or until reduced by half.

3. Cook half of ribs in 2 Tbsp. hot oil in a large skillet over medium-high heat 3 minutes on each side or until browned. Repeat with remaining oil and ribs. Remove from heat, discard drippings, and wipe skillet clean.

4. Pour wine and brandy into skillet and return to medium heat. Bring wine and brandy to a boil; boil 5 minutes or until reduced by half. Stir wine mixture into reduced stock.

5. Place ribs in a large Dutch oven. Add tomatoes and next 5 ingredients, nestling them around the ribs; add parsley, thyme, and rosemary sprigs. Pour stock mixture into Dutch oven; simmer over high heat. Place a piece of parchment paper directly on beef, and cover Dutch oven with a tight-fitting lid.

6. Bake at 300° for 3½ to 4 hours or until meat is tender and pulls away from bone.

7. Let ribs stand in Dutch oven at room temperature 30 minutes. Remove parchment paper. Carefully transfer to a serving platter; cover with parchment paper or aluminum foil. Skim fat from cooking liquid, and pour liquid through a fine wire-mesh strainer into a large saucepan; discard solids. Bring to a simmer over medium-high heat. Simmer, whisking occasionally, 5 minutes or until sauce reduces slightly. Remove from heat; whisk in butter until it melts and sauce is smooth. Serve sauce with ribs.

Note: We tested with Swanson Unsalted Beef Cooking Stock.

Brisket with Mushroom-and-Onion Gravy

Flat-cut brisket comes in a range of sizes. If you get a large, oblong piece,
trim the thin end off, if necessary, so it will fit in a Dutch oven and cook evenly.

MAKES: 10 TO 12 SERVINGS   HANDS-ON: 1 HOUR 15 MIN.   TOTAL: 13 HOURS 45 MIN.

2	Tbsp. kosher salt	12	garlic cloves, smashed
1	Tbsp. garlic powder	2	large carrots, cut into 1-inch pieces
2½	tsp. freshly ground black pepper	2	fresh thyme sprigs
1	tsp. onion powder	¼	bunch fresh flat-leaf parsley
1	(5-lb.) beef brisket, trimmed	3	large yellow onions, divided
Parchment paper		6	Tbsp. butter, divided
1	(1-oz.) package dried porcini mushrooms	1	lb. whole cremini mushrooms, quartered
2	cups boiling water	2½	Tbsp. cornstarch
2	Tbsp. olive oil		Garnish: coarsely chopped fresh flat-leaf parsley
2	cups reduced-sodium beef broth		

1. Stir together first 4 ingredients. Rub mixture over both sides of brisket. Place brisket in a parchment paper-lined jelly-roll pan; cover and chill 8 hours.

2. Let brisket stand at room temperature 30 minutes. Preheat oven to 325°. Soak dried porcini mushrooms in 2 cups boiling water 10 minutes.

3. Meanwhile, cook brisket in hot oil in a large Dutch oven 4 minutes on each side or until browned. Add broth, next 4 ingredients, porcini mushrooms, and mushroom soaking liquid to Dutch oven. Cut 1 onion into wedges, and add to Dutch oven. Place a piece of parchment paper directly on brisket, and cover Dutch oven with a tight-fitting lid.

4. Bake at 325° for 4 hours or until brisket is fork-tender. Let stand, covered with parchment and lid, in Dutch oven at room temperature for 30 minutes. Discard parchment paper.

5. Meanwhile, thinly slice remaining 2 onions. Melt 2 Tbsp. butter in a large skillet over medium heat. Add onion slices, and cook, stirring occasionally, 15 minutes or until golden and tender. Remove from skillet.

6. Increase heat to medium-high; melt 2 Tbsp. butter in skillet. Add cremini mushrooms, and sauté 8 minutes or until browned and tender. Remove cremini mushrooms from skillet; add to onion mixture.

7. Remove brisket to a cutting board, and slice across the grain. Transfer slices to a serving platter, and cover loosely to keep warm. Pour cooking liquid through a fine wire-mesh strainer into a medium saucepan; discard solids. Bring liquid to a boil over medium-high heat. Stir in onion-mushroom mixture, and cook, stirring occasionally, 5 minutes.

8. Melt remaining 2 Tbsp. butter in a small saucepan over medium-high heat; add cornstarch, and whisk until smooth. Cook mixture, whisking constantly, 30 seconds. Add cornstarch mixture to gravy; whisk to combine. Bring gravy to a boil, whisking occasionally. Cook gravy, whisking constantly, 1 minute. Remove from heat; add kosher salt and freshly ground black pepper to taste. Serve gravy over brisket. Garnish, if desired.

Note: We tested with Swanson 50% Less Sodium Beef Broth.

Perfect Beef Tenderloin

When seasoning roasts, this will generally do the trick: 1 tsp. of kosher salt per pound of meat.

MAKES: 8 SERVINGS HANDS-ON: 10 MIN. TOTAL: 50 MIN.

1	(5- to 7-lb.) beef tenderloin, trimmed	5	to 7 tsp. kosher salt
3	Tbsp. butter, softened	¾	tsp. cracked black pepper

1. Preheat oven to 425°. Place beef on a wire rack in a jelly-roll pan. Rub butter over beef, and sprinkle with salt and pepper.
2. Bake at 425° for 25 to 35 minutes or until a meat thermometer inserted into thickest portion registers 135° (medium rare). Cover loosely with aluminum foil and let stand 15 minutes before slicing.

Note: We tested with Diamond Crystal Kosher Salt.

Homemade Hot Mustard

In Greenville, Mississippi, this mustard is golden.
It's been passed from one kitchen to another for decades.

MAKES: 2 ¼ CUPS HANDS-ON: 20 MIN. TOTAL: 13 HOURS 20 MIN.

1	cup dry mustard	1	cup sugar
1	cup apple cider vinegar	3	large pasteurized eggs, lightly beaten

1. Stir together first 2 ingredients in top of a double boiler. Cover and let stand 12 to 24 hours.
2. Pour water to depth of 1 inch into bottom of a double boiler over medium-high heat; bring to a boil. Reduce heat to low, and simmer; place top of double boiler over simmering water. Whisk sugar and eggs into mustard mixture, and cook, whisking constantly, 8 to 10 minutes or until thickened. Remove from heat, and cool completely (about 1 hour). (Mixture will continue to thicken as it cools.) Refrigerate in an airtight container up to 2 weeks.

Note: We tested with Colman's Mustard Powder.

Horseradish Sauce

Give this classic tenderloin condiment as much horseradish oomph as you please.

MAKES: ABOUT 2 CUPS HANDS-ON: 5 MIN. TOTAL: 5 MIN.

1 ⅓	cups sour cream	1 ½	tsp. Dijon mustard
½	cup whipping cream, whipped to soft peaks	2	to 3 tsp. fresh lemon juice
6	Tbsp. prepared horseradish	½	tsp. sugar

Fold together first 4 ingredients in a medium bowl. Stir in lemon juice and sugar. Add salt and pepper to taste.

Company Pot Roast with Creamy Mushroom Grits

*Bacon, garlic, and red wine imbue humble chuck roast with robust character
and rich beef-bourguignon flavor as the meat transforms in the slow cooker.
Serve sliced or in chunks over Creamy Mushroom Grits.*

MAKES: 6 SERVINGS HANDS-ON: 40 MIN. TOTAL: 9 HOURS, INCLUDING GRITS

---

6 medium leeks	1 cup dry red wine
4 thick bacon slices	⅓ cup balsamic vinegar
1 (4- to 4 ½-lb.) boneless chuck roast, trimmed	1 lb. carrots, cut into 4-inch sticks
2 tsp. freshly ground black pepper	1 lb. parsnips, cut into 4-inch sticks
1½ tsp. kosher salt	1 cup chicken broth
2 Tbsp. olive oil	1 Tbsp. cornstarch
3 garlic cloves, minced	Creamy Mushroom Grits (recipe below)
⅓ cup firmly packed light brown sugar	Garnish: fresh flat-leaf parsley sprigs

1. Lightly grease a 5- to 6-qt. slow cooker with cooking spray. Remove and discard root ends and dark green tops of leeks. Cut a slit lengthwise, and rinse thoroughly under cold running water to remove grit and sand. Place leeks in slow cooker.

2. Cook bacon in a large skillet over medium heat 6 to 8 minutes or until crisp. Remove bacon, and drain on paper towels, reserving 3 Tbsp. hot drippings in skillet. Crumble bacon.

3. Sprinkle roast with pepper and salt. Add olive oil to hot drippings in skillet. Place roast in skillet, and cook over medium-high heat 2 to 3 minutes on each side or until browned. Transfer roast to slow cooker, reserving 1 Tbsp. drippings in skillet.

4. Add garlic to hot drippings, and sauté 30 seconds. Add brown sugar, stirring until sugar melts. Add wine and balsamic vinegar, and cook 2 minutes, stirring to loosen particles from bottom of skillet. Pour mixture over roast, and top with carrots and parsnips.

5. Cover and cook on LOW 8 to 10 hours or until meat shreds easily with a fork.

6. Transfer roast to a cutting board; cut into large chunks, removing any large pieces of fat. Transfer roast and vegetables to a platter, and keep warm.

7. Skim fat from juices in slow cooker, and transfer juices to a 2-qt. saucepan. Add broth, and bring to a boil over medium-high heat. Stir together cornstarch and 2 Tbsp. water in a small bowl until smooth; add to pan, stirring until blended. Boil 1 minute. Add salt and pepper to taste. Serve gravy with roast and vegetables over Creamy Mushroom Grits. Top with crumbled bacon. Garnish, if desired.

Creamy Mushroom Grits

This mushroom-laden side dish serves as a savory base to pot roast.

¼ cup butter	½ cup freshly grated Parmesan cheese
2 (3.5-oz.) packages shiitake mushrooms, stemmed and sliced	1 tsp. kosher salt
	½ tsp. freshly ground black pepper
1 cup uncooked quick-cooking yellow grits	¼ cup chopped fresh flat-leaf parsley

Melt butter in a medium skillet over medium-high heat; add mushrooms. Sauté 3 to 4 minutes or until mushrooms begin to brown. Prepare grits according to package directions. Stir in Parmesan cheese, kosher salt, and pepper. Stir in mushrooms and parsley. Makes 6 servings.

Slow-Cooker Sunday Sauce

MAKES: 8 ½ CUPS HANDS-ON: 1 HOUR 10 MIN. TOTAL: 9 HOURS 10 MIN.

3   lb. boneless pork shoulder, cut into 2-inch cubes
1 ½   tsp. kosher salt
1   tsp. ground black pepper
3   Tbsp. olive oil, divided
1   lb. sweet Italian sausage, casings removed, chopped
4   oz. pancetta, chopped
2 ¾   cups chopped yellow onion
1   cup chopped carrots
8   garlic cloves, chopped

1   cup red wine
1   (28-oz.) can whole peeled tomatoes, chopped
1   (28-oz.) can tomato puree
3   fresh thyme sprigs
2   fresh oregano sprigs
1   fresh rosemary sprig
½   cup reduced-sodium chicken broth
Hot cooked pasta
Garnishes: shaved Parmesan cheese, fresh basil, sliced

1. Stir together first 3 ingredients; sauté, in batches, in 2 Tbsp. hot oil in a large skillet over medium-high heat 10 minutes. Transfer to an 8-qt. slow cooker.

2. Sauté sausage in remaining 1 Tbsp. hot oil in skillet 6 minutes or until no longer pink. Transfer to slow cooker, reserving drippings in skillet.

3. Sauté pancetta in hot drippings in skillet over medium heat 7 minutes or until crisp. Add onion, carrots, and garlic; sauté 5 minutes or until tender. Increase heat to high; add wine. Bring to a boil, stirring to loosen browned bits. Cook, stirring constantly, 5 minutes or until reduced by half.

4. Add tomatoes and tomato puree; bring to a boil. Transfer to slow cooker; add thyme and next 3 ingredients. Cover; cook on HIGH 1 hour. Reduce heat to LOW; cook 7 hours. Discard herbs; stir hot cooked pasta into sauce. Garnish, if desired.

*Canned whole peeled tomatoes
work best in this delicious sauce.
Use a pair of kitchen shears
to coarsely cut them in the can,
or squeeze them by hand.*

Spinach Lasagna

MAKES: 6 TO 8 SERVINGS HANDS-ON: 50 MIN. TOTAL: 2 HOURS 35 MIN.

1	(24-oz.) jar pasta sauce	⅓	cup olive oil
¼	tsp. dried crushed red pepper	8	garlic cloves, minced
2 ⅓	cups heavy cream, divided	2	(10-oz.) packages fresh baby spinach
32	oz. ricotta cheese	2	Tbsp. butter
1	oz. fresh basil, chopped	1	Tbsp. all-purpose flour
½	tsp. kosher salt	12	no-boil lasagna noodles
2	cups freshly shredded Parmesan cheese, divided	1	(12-oz.) jar roasted red bell pepper strips, drained
4	large shallots, thinly sliced		

1. Preheat oven to 350°. Combine first 2 ingredients and 1 cup cream. Separately combine ricotta, next 2 ingredients, and 1 cup Parmesan. Sauté shallots in hot oil in a Dutch oven over medium-high heat 3 minutes. Add garlic; sauté 1 minute. Remove shallot mixture.

2. Add one-third of spinach to Dutch oven; cook over medium-high heat 1 minute or until wilted. Place spinach in a colander; drain. Repeat with remaining spinach.

3. Cook butter and flour in Dutch oven over medium heat, stirring constantly, 1 minute. Add 1 ⅓ cups cream; bring to a boil. Remove from heat; add spinach and shallots.

4. Coat a 13- x 9-inch baking dish with cooking spray. Pour ½ cup sauce mixture in baking dish; top with 3 lasagna noodles. Layer half of spinach mixture, half of roasted peppers, 3 lasagna noodles, and half of ricotta mixture over pasta. Repeat layers, beginning with spinach mixture; top with 3 lasagna noodles. Pour remaining sauce mixture over top. Place baking dish on an aluminum foil-lined baking sheet.

5. Bake at 350° for 1 hour. Top with 1 cup Parmesan, and bake 15 minutes. Let stand 30 minutes before serving.

Always a crowd-pleaser, this lasagna is layered with hearty veggies— spinach, roasted red peppers, and lots of garlic, shallots, and basil.

Chicken Enchiladas

MAKE AHEAD TIP

Make the enchilada sauce up to 3 days ahead; the flavors will meld and only get better.

SAUCE

4	Anaheim peppers or 3 large jalapeño peppers
3	poblano peppers
6	plum tomatoes, halved
1	onion, cut into wedges
7	garlic cloves, unpeeled
1	(28-oz.) can tomato sauce
2	cups chicken broth
1	Tbsp. ground chipotle chile pepper
1	Tbsp. chili powder
1	tsp. ground cumin
1	tsp. dried oregano
1½	tsp. kosher salt, divided

ENCHILADAS

1	(8-oz.) block Monterey Jack cheese
12	(6-inch) corn tortillas
4	cups shredded deli-roasted chicken
½	(8-oz.) block sharp Cheddar cheese, shredded
2	avocados, chopped
½	cup torn fresh cilantro leaves
2	Tbsp. fresh lime juice

1. Prepare Sauce: Preheat broiler with oven rack 5 inches from heat. Broil first 5 ingredients on an aluminum foil-lined baking sheet 6 minutes or until peppers blister and char. Remove from oven; let stand 10 minutes or until cool enough to handle. Peel and seed peppers; peel garlic. Reduce oven temperature to 375°.

2. Bring tomato sauce, next 5 ingredients, broiled vegetables, and 1 tsp. salt to a boil in a large saucepan over high heat, stirring occasionally. Reduce heat to medium-low; cook, stirring occasionally, 35 minutes. Remove from heat; cool 10 minutes. Process with a handheld blender or in batches in a food processor or blender until smooth.

3. Prepare Enchiladas: Shred 2 oz. Monterey Jack cheese to yield ½ cup. Cut remaining Monterey Jack cheese into 12 (4- x ½-inch) sticks.

4. Lightly grease a 13- x 9-inch baking dish with cooking spray. Spread 1 cup enchilada sauce in baking dish. Spread a thin layer of sauce on 1 tortilla. Place ⅓ cup chicken and 1 Monterey Jack cheese stick on edge of tortilla, and roll tortilla. Place in baking dish, seam side down. Repeat with remaining tortillas, chicken, and cheese sticks. Pour 2 ½ cups sauce over tortillas. Chill remaining sauce for another use. Bake enchiladas at 375° for 30 minutes.

5. Top enchiladas with shredded Cheddar and shredded Monterey Jack cheese; bake 5 more minutes or until cheese is melted. Remove from oven; let stand 10 minutes.

6. Meanwhile, combine avocado, next 2 ingredients, and remaining ½ tsp. salt; serve with enchiladas.

BREAD BASKET

Turn your kitchen into a holiday bakery with this tempting selection of biscuits, rolls, and breads

Spoon Bread
Corn Muffins

Spoon Bread Corn Muffins

*These light and airy muffins have a very fine, almost custardy texture from
the fine grind of the cornmeal. Serve with extra butter and honey.*

MAKES: 1 DOZEN HANDS-ON: 15 MIN. TOTAL: 40 MIN.

1½ cups finely ground white cornmeal
1   tsp. baking soda
1   tsp. kosher salt
2   large eggs, lightly beaten

2¼ cups buttermilk
¼   cup freshly grated sharp Cheddar cheese
1   Tbsp. chopped fresh chives
Unsalted butter

1. Preheat oven to 425°. Combine first 3 ingredients in a large bowl. Whisk eggs and buttermilk into cornmeal mixture, stirring vigorously until smooth. Stir in cheese and chives. Pour batter into a greased (with unsalted butter) 12-cup muffin pan.
2. Bake at 425° for 13 minutes or until lightly browned. Cool in pan on a wire rack 5 minutes. Remove from pan to rack; cool 5 minutes.

Zucchini-Bacon Spoon Bread

MAKES: 8 SERVINGS HANDS-ON: 10 MIN. TOTAL: 1 HOUR 10 MIN.

2   cups milk
1   Tbsp. sugar
1   tsp. table salt
½   tsp. freshly ground pepper
⅛   tsp. ground red pepper

1   cup plain yellow cornmeal
2   cups shredded zucchini
1   cup shredded sharp Cheddar cheese
8   cooked bacon slices, crumbled
2   large eggs, separated

1. Preheat oven to 375°. Bring first 5 ingredients to a simmer in a large heavy saucepan over medium-high heat (do not boil); gradually whisk in cornmeal. Cook, stirring constantly, 1 minute or until thick and smooth. Remove from heat, and stir in zucchini, cheese, and bacon. Stir in egg yolks until blended.
2. Grease a 1½-qt. soufflé dish or deep baking dish with cooking spray. Beat egg whites at high speed with an electric mixer until stiff peaks form. Stir one-third of egg white mixture into cornmeal mixture. Spoon into soufflé dish.
3. Bake at 375° for 46 to 50 minutes or until top is lightly browned. Serve immediately.

Egg Bread

MAKES: **6 TO 8 SERVINGS** HANDS-ON: **30 MIN.** TOTAL: **55 MIN.**

1   cup milk
2 ¼ cups plain yellow cornmeal, divided
3   large eggs
1   tsp. table salt

2   cups buttermilk
1   tsp. baking soda
2   Tbsp. shortening

1. Preheat oven to 400°.
2. Stir together milk and 1 cup water in a large saucepan. Bring to a boil over high heat. Remove from heat, and gradually whisk in 2 cups cornmeal. Let stand until needed.
3. Beat eggs in a large bowl at high speed with an electric mixer until foamy. Add salt, and beat 5 minutes or until mixture is light and fluffy.
4. Stir together buttermilk and baking soda in a small bowl. Pour into egg mixture, and mix well. Add cornmeal mixture, and stir until smooth.
5. Place shortening in a 10-inch cast-iron skillet. Place skillet in oven 5 minutes. Pour melted shortening into cornmeal mixture, and mix well. Stir in remaining ¼ cup cornmeal. Pour mixture into hot skillet.
6. Bake at 400° for 25 to 30 minutes or until firm. Remove from skillet immediately, and serve hot.

To many people, the term "egg bread" refers to yeast bread that is similar to challah or brioche.

Rosemary Focaccia

Pair this flavorful bread with your favorite pesto for a mouthwatering appetizer.

MAKES: 10 TO 12 SERVINGS HANDS-ON: 30 MIN. TOTAL: 3 HOURS

1 (¼-oz.) envelope active dry yeast
1 ⅔ cups warm water (100° to 110°)
4 ½ cups bread flour
¼ cup extra virgin olive oil

1 Tbsp. table salt
2 Tbsp. fresh rosemary leaves, divided
3 Tbsp. extra virgin olive oil
1 tsp. kosher salt

1. Stir together yeast and warm water (100° to 110°) in bowl of a heavy-duty electric stand mixer; let stand 5 minutes.

2. Add bread flour, ¼ cup oil, and 1 Tbsp. table salt to yeast mixture. Beat on low speed, using paddle attachment, 10 seconds or until blended. Increase speed to medium. Beat 45 seconds or until dough is smooth. Add 1 Tbsp. rosemary. Replace paddle attachment with dough hook; increase speed to medium-high, and beat 4 minutes. (Dough will be sticky.)

3. Grease a large bowl with cooking spray. Turn dough out onto a floured surface, and knead until smooth and elastic (about 1 minute). Place in bowl, turning to coat. Cover dough with plastic wrap, and let rise in a warm place (80° to 85°), free from drafts, 1 hour or until doubled in bulk.

4. Grease a 15- x 10-inch jelly-roll pan with cooking spray. Place dough in pan, pressing to about ¼-inch thickness. Cover with a kitchen towel, and let rise in a warm place 1 hour.

5. Preheat oven to 475°. Press handle of a wooden spoon into dough to make indentations at 1-inch intervals; drizzle with 3 Tbsp. oil. Sprinkle with kosher salt and remaining 1 Tbsp. rosemary. Bake 14 to 16 minutes or until top is light brown. Remove from pan to a wire rack, and cool 10 minutes.

Grape Focaccia

Don't be intimidated by homemade bread; even a beginner can master this simple baking sheet focaccia. It's an effortlessly gorgeous dish for entertaining, and the unexpected combination of sweet and savory flavors will impress.

MAKES: 12 TO 14 SERVINGS   HANDS-ON: 30 MIN.   TOTAL: 3 HOURS

1   (¼-oz.) envelope active dry yeast
1 ⅔   cups warm water (100° to 110°)
4 ½   cups bread flour
1 ½   Tbsp. kosher salt
¾   cup olive oil, divided
2   Tbsp. chopped fresh thyme

1   Tbsp. chopped fresh rosemary
1   lb. red and green grapes, halved
Coarse salt
Freshly ground black pepper
Garnish: chopped fresh rosemary

1. Stir together yeast and warm water (100° to 110°) in bowl of a heavy-duty electric stand mixer; let stand 5 minutes. Add bread flour, salt, and ¼ cup oil to yeast mixture; beat on low speed, using paddle attachment, 25 seconds or until blended. Add chopped herbs. Switch to dough hook; increase speed to medium-high, and beat 5 minutes. (Dough will be sticky.)
2. Grease a large bowl well with cooking spray. Place dough in bowl, turning to grease top. Cover with plastic wrap, and let rise in a warm place (80° to 85°), free from drafts, 1 hour or until doubled in bulk.
3. Drizzle ¼ cup olive oil in a half-sheet pan or jelly-roll pan; place dough in pan. Press dough down and into edges of pan, using your fingers. (It's okay if there are holes in the dough.) Cover with plastic wrap, and let rise in warm place 1 hour.
4. Preheat oven to 425°. Scatter grapes over dough. Drizzle with remaining ¼ cup olive oil, and sprinkle with coarse salt and freshly ground black pepper. Bake 30 to 35 minutes or until golden brown. Serve warm or at room temperature. Garnish, if desired.

As an appetizer, serve the warm slab of bread, sliced, on a large cutting board with a few wedges of your favorite cheese. Try muscadines or figs in place of the grapes. For leftovers, spread the focaccia with peanut butter for a fresh, sophisticated spin on PB&J.

Perfect Cornbread

Perfect Cornbread

Our Test Kitchen granted the "perfect" moniker to Ben Mims' recipe, developed for a recent issue, thanks to the extra flavor and superior texture browned butter affords.

MAKES: 8 TO 10 SERVINGS   HANDS-ON: 20 MIN.   TOTAL: 45 MIN.

1	cup plain yellow cornmeal	¼	tsp. baking soda
1	cup all-purpose flour	2	cups buttermilk
1	Tbsp. baking powder	2	large eggs
1	tsp. kosher salt	½	cup butter

1. Preheat oven to 425°. Whisk together first 5 ingredients in a large bowl. Whisk together buttermilk and eggs; stir into cornmeal mixture just until combined. Heat a 10-inch cast-iron skillet over medium-high heat until it just begins to smoke. Add butter, and stir until butter is melted. Stir melted butter into cornbread batter. Pour batter into hot skillet.

2. Bake at 425° for 25 to 30 minutes or until golden and cornbread pulls away from sides of skillet. Invert cornbread onto a wire rack; serve warm.

Cornbread Biscuits

MAKES: 15 BISCUITS   HANDS-ON: 30 MIN.   TOTAL: 53 MIN.

3	cups self-rising soft-wheat flour	1½	cups buttermilk
½	cup self-rising yellow cornmeal mix	1	tsp. plain yellow cornmeal
¼	cup cold butter, cut into pieces	2	Tbsp. butter, melted
¼	cup shortening, cut into pieces		

1. Preheat oven to 500°. Whisk together first 2 ingredients in a large bowl. Cut in cold butter and shortening with a pastry blender until mixture resembles small peas and dough is crumbly. Cover and chill 10 minutes. Add buttermilk, stirring just until dry ingredients are moistened.

2. Turn dough out onto a heavily floured surface; knead 3 or 4 times. Pat the dough into a ¾-inch-thick circle.

3. Cut dough with a well-floured 2 ½-inch round cutter, rerolling scraps as needed. Sprinkle cornmeal on ungreased baking sheets; place biscuits on baking sheets. Lightly brush tops with 2 Tbsp. melted butter.

4. Bake at 500° for 13 to 15 minutes or until golden brown.

Mrs. Monty's Rolls

MAKES: **ABOUT 3 DOZEN** HANDS-ON: **40 MIN.** TOTAL: **4 HOURS 10 MIN.**

1 (¼-oz.) envelope active dry yeast
2 cups warm water (100° to 110°)
½ cup sugar
3 Tbsp. shortening, softened
1 tsp. table salt

1 large egg, lightly beaten
6 to 6 ½ cups sifted all-purpose flour
3 Tbsp. butter, softened
2 Tbsp. butter, melted
Chopped fresh herbs (optional)

1. Combine yeast and warm water (100° to 110°) in a large bowl; let stand 5 minutes. Stir in sugar and next 3 ingredients. Whisk in 3 cups sifted flour, 1 cup at a time, until combined. Gradually stir in more flour to make a soft dough (about 3 to 3 ½ cups). Using floured hands, shape dough into a smooth ball. Grease a bowl well with cooking spray. Place dough in bowl, turning to grease top. Cover with plastic wrap. Let rise in a warm place (80° to 85°) 2 hours or until doubled in bulk.

2. Lightly grease 2 baking sheets with cooking spray. Punch dough down. Turn dough out onto a floured surface, and roll to ½-inch thickness. Cut with a 3-inch round cutter, rerolling scraps once. Lightly press each round into a 4-inch oval. Spread ¼ tsp. softened butter on half of each oval. Fold unbuttered half over to form a half-moon shape; place 2 inches apart on baking sheets. Cover and let rise in a warm place 40 minutes or until doubled in bulk.

3. Preheat oven to 375°. Bake, in batches, 14 to 15 minutes or until golden brown. Transfer to a wire rack; brush with melted butter with chopped fresh herbs stirred in, if desired.

These springy rolls are just the thing for sandwiching ham and stacking with a colorful array of condiments.

Graham Cracker Rolls

The graham cracker crumbs give these rolls an added flavor that will make them very popular with your family and friends.

MAKES: **ABOUT 2 DOZEN** HANDS-ON: **35 MIN.** TOTAL: **9 HOURS 35 MIN.**

1 (¼-oz.) envelope active dry yeast
½ cup warm water (100° to 110°)
¼ cup plus 2 ½ tsp. sugar, divided
1 large egg
¼ cup shortening
1 tsp. table salt

½ cup boiling water
2 ½ cups all-purpose flour
¾ cup graham cracker crumbs, divided
Parchment paper
3 Tbsp. butter, melted

1. Combine first 2 ingredients and 1 tsp. sugar; let stand 5 minutes.
2. Beat egg, shortening, salt, and ¼ cup sugar at medium speed with a heavy-duty electric stand mixer until creamy. Add boiling water; stir until shortening melts. Stir in yeast mixture. Stir flour and ½ cup cracker crumbs into egg mixture.
3. Place dough in a lightly greased (with shortening) bowl; cover and chill 8 to 24 hours.
4. Punch dough down. Turn dough out onto a lightly floured surface, and knead 4 or 5 times. Roll to ½-inch thickness. Cut dough into rounds with a 1 ½- to 2-inch round cutter, rerolling scraps twice. Place rolls 1 inch apart on a parchment paper-lined baking sheet, and brush with melted butter.
5. Stir together remaining ¼ cup crumbs and 1 ½ tsp. sugar. Sprinkle mixture over rolls. Cover and let rise in a warm place (80° to 85°), free from drafts, 45 minutes to 1 hour or until doubled in bulk.
6. Preheat oven to 350°. Bake, uncovered, 15 to 18 minutes or until golden.

Angel Biscuits

MAKES: **ABOUT 2 DOZEN** HANDS-ON: **30 MIN.** TOTAL: **2 HOURS 50 MIN.**

½   cup warm water (100° to 110°)
1   (¼-oz.) envelope active dry yeast
1   tsp. sugar
5   cups all-purpose flour
3   Tbsp. sugar
5   tsp. baking powder
1½ tsp. table salt

1   tsp. baking soda
½   cup cold butter, cubed
½   cup shortening, cubed
2   cups buttermilk
Parchment paper
¼   cup butter, melted and divided

1. Stir together first 3 ingredients in a small bowl. Let stand 5 minutes.
2. Stir together flour and next 4 ingredients in a large bowl; cut butter and shortening into flour mixture with a pastry blender or 2 forks until crumbly. Add yeast mixture and buttermilk to flour mixture, stirring just until dry ingredients are moistened. Cover bowl with plastic wrap, and chill 2 hours to 5 days.
3. Preheat oven to 400°. Turn dough out onto a lightly floured surface, and knead 3 or 4 times. Gently roll dough into a ¾-inch-thick circle, and fold dough in half; repeat. Gently roll dough to ¾-inch thickness; cut with a 2-inch round cutter. Reroll remaining scraps, and cut with cutter. Place rounds, with sides touching, in a 10- or 12-inch cast-iron skillet or on a parchment paper-lined baking sheet. Brush biscuits with 2 Tbsp. melted butter.
4. Bake at 400° for 15 to 20 minutes or until golden brown. Brush with remaining melted butter, and serve.

Nestle these yeast biscuits snugly together in the pan and they'll rise even higher when baked. You don't have to use all the dough at once—refrigerate in an airtight container up to 5 days.

Herbed Potato Flake Rolls

Like magic, packaged potato flakes give these fluffy beauties a lighter-than-air texture that makes them perfect for sopping up gravy. Trust us, they go fast.

MAKES: ABOUT 4 ½ DOZEN HANDS-ON: 45 MIN. TOTAL: 2 HOURS 50 MIN.

1 ½ **cups buttermilk**	1 **tsp. sugar**
⅔ **cup sugar**	1 **large egg, lightly beaten**
⅓ **cup butter**	4 ½ **cups bread flour, divided**
½ **cup instant potato flakes**	½ **cup butter, melted**
1 ¾ **tsp. table salt**	2 **tsp. chopped fresh rosemary**
1 **tsp. baking soda**	**Parchment paper**
2 **(¼-oz.) envelopes active dry yeast**	**Garnish: fresh rosemary sprigs**
½ **cup warm water (100° to 110°)**	

1. Stir together first 6 ingredients in a small saucepan, and cook over medium-low heat, stirring constantly, 3 minutes or until butter melts. Cool about 15 minutes or until the temperature reaches 110°.

2. Stir together yeast and next 2 ingredients; let stand 5 minutes.

3. Beat buttermilk mixture and yeast mixture at low speed with a heavy-duty electric stand mixer until blended. Add egg, and beat just until blended. Gradually add 4 cups flour, beating at low speed 4 to 6 minutes or until blended and dough is soft and smooth.

4. Turn dough out onto a lightly floured surface, and knead, adding up to ½ cup more flour, 1 Tbsp. at a time, as needed, until dough is smooth and elastic (about 5 minutes). Place dough in a large bowl coated with cooking spray, turning to grease top.

5. Cover and let rise in a warm place (80° to 85°), free from drafts, 1 hour or until doubled in bulk.

6. Stir together melted butter and rosemary. Punch dough down. Turn dough out onto floured surface, and roll into a 22- x 15-inch rectangle. Brush dough with half of butter mixture. (Keep remaining butter mixture at room temperature.)

7. Cut dough into 11 (2- x 15-inch) strips. Cut each strip into 5 (3- x 2-inch) rectangles. Make a crease across each rectangle by pressing lightly with a knife, and fold in half. Place rolls 2 inches apart on 2 parchment paper-lined baking sheets. Cover and let rise in a warm place (80° to 85°), free from drafts, 30 to 45 minutes or until doubled in bulk.

8. Preheat oven to 350°. Bake, uncovered, 15 to 18 minutes or until golden brown. Brush with remaining butter mixture, and serve immediately. Garnish, if desired.

TREATS FOR EARLY RISERS

*Celebrate the magic of the morning
with a table full of delicious breads, casseroles,
and other breakfast favorites*

Brie-and-Sausage Breakfast Casserole

Brie-and-Sausage Breakfast Casserole

MAKES: 8 TO 10 SERVINGS HANDS-ON: 30 MIN. TOTAL: 9 HOURS 30 MIN.

1 (8-oz.) Brie round*	1 Tbsp. chopped fresh sage or 1 tsp. dried rubbed sage
1 lb. hot ground pork sausage	
6 white sandwich bread slices	1 tsp. seasoned salt
1 cup grated Parmesan cheese	1 tsp. dry mustard
7 large eggs, divided	Garnishes: chopped green onions, grated Parmesan cheese
3 cups whipping cream, divided	
2 cups fat-free milk	

1. Trim rind from Brie, and discard; cut cheese into cubes, and set aside.

2. Cook sausage in a large skillet over medium-high heat, stirring until it crumbles and is no longer pink; drain well.

3. Cut crusts from bread slices, and place crusts evenly in bottom of a lightly greased 13- x 9-inch baking dish. Layer evenly with bread slices, sausage, Brie, and Parmesan cheese.

4. Whisk together 5 eggs, 2 cups whipping cream, and next 4 ingredients; pour evenly over cheeses. Cover and chill 8 hours.

5. Preheat oven to 350°. Whisk together remaining 2 eggs and remaining 1 cup whipping cream; pour evenly over chilled mixture.

6. Bake at 350° for 1 hour or until casserole is set. Garnish, if desired.

* 2 cups (8 oz.) shredded Swiss cheese may be substituted.

Sausage and Egg Casserole

MAKES: 8 TO 10 SERVINGS HANDS-ON: 30 MIN. TOTAL: 1 HOUR 30 MIN.

8 (1½-oz.) sourdough bread slices, cut into ½-inch cubes	4 large eggs
	1 Tbsp. Dijon mustard
1 (12-oz.) package fully cooked pork sausage patties, chopped	½ cup buttermilk
	1 (10¾-oz.) can cream of mushroom soup
2½ cups 2% reduced-fat milk	1 cup (4 oz.) shredded sharp Cheddar cheese

1. Preheat oven to 350°. Lightly grease 2 (8-inch) square baking dishes or 1 (13- x 9-inch) baking dish with cooking spray. Arrange bread in baking dishes. Top evenly with sausage. Whisk together 2½ cups milk, eggs, and Dijon mustard. Pour over bread mixture.

2. Whisk together buttermilk and cream of mushroom soup. Spoon over bread mixture; sprinkle with Cheddar cheese. Place casserole on a baking sheet.

3. Bake at 350° for 1 hour or until casserole is set. Serve immediately.

MAKE AHEAD TIP

Cover an unbaked casserole with plastic wrap, then foil, and freeze up to 1 month. Thaw overnight in the refrigerator. Bake as directed.

Cheesy Sausage-and-Croissant Casserole

MAKES **8 TO 10 SERVINGS** HANDS-ON: **20 MIN.** TOTAL: **9 HOURS 15 MIN.**

1   lb. hot ground pork sausage
     (such as Jimmy Dean)
1¼ cups (5 oz.) shredded Parmesan cheese
1   tsp. table salt
6   green onions, sliced
1   (13.22-oz.) package mini croissants
     (about 24), torn

3   cups milk
1   cup heavy cream
5   large eggs, lightly beaten
2   cups (8 oz.) shredded Gruyère cheese
Garnishes: sliced green onions, freshly
     ground pepper

1. Grease a 13- x 9-inch baking dish with cooking spray. Cook sausage 8 minutes in a skillet over medium-high heat, stirring to crumble. Toss together sausage, Parmesan, and next 3 ingredients; arrange in baking dish.
2. Whisk together milk and next 2 ingredients; pour over sausage mixture. Cover and chill 8 hours.
3. Preheat oven to 350°. Uncover casserole, and sprinkle with Gruyère. Bake 45 minutes or until golden. Let stand 10 minutes. Garnish, if desired.

This casserole is rich, delicious, and worthy of Christmas breakfast. Gruyère cheese browns beautifully and adds a nutty flavor to the dish. You can sub Swiss cheese, if you prefer.

Carolina Gold Rice Grits and Eggs

MAKES: **4 TO 6 SERVINGS** HANDS-ON: **40 MIN.** TOTAL: **55 MIN.**

4	fresh thyme sprigs	1½	tsp. kosher salt
2	fresh rosemary sprigs	½	cup uncooked rice grits
1	bay leaf	6	bacon slices
½	tsp. black peppercorns	6	large eggs
	Cheesecloth	1	tsp. dry mustard
	Kitchen string	5	green onions, sliced
1	Tbsp. curry powder		

1. Place first 4 ingredients in a 6-inch square of cheesecloth; tie with kitchen string. Bring 5 cups water to a boil in a 3½-qt. saucepan over medium-high heat. Add curry powder, salt, and cheesecloth bundle. Stir in rice grits, and cook 5 to 7 minutes or until slightly tender. Remove cheesecloth bundle. Drain rice grits, and let stand 10 to 15 minutes or until very dry.

2. Meanwhile, cook bacon in a medium nonstick skillet over medium-high heat 8 to 10 minutes or until crisp; remove bacon, and drain on paper towels, reserving 3 Tbsp. drippings in skillet. Crumble bacon.

3. Whisk together eggs, mustard, and 1 tsp. water.

4. Add rice grits to hot drippings, and cook over medium-high heat, stirring constantly, 8 to 10 minutes or until grits are crisp and tender. Reduce heat to medium-low. Add egg mixture to skillet, and cook, without stirring, 2 to 3 minutes or until eggs begin to set on bottom. Gently draw cooked edges away from sides of skillet. Stir in bacon and green onions, and cook 5 to 7 minutes or until eggs are thickened and moist. Add salt and pepper to taste; serve immediately.

Note: We tested with Anson Mills Carolina Gold Rice Grits.

The texture of rice grits will remind you of risotto, which makes them perfect for pairing with recipes that have sauces.

Bacon-and-Cheddar Grits Quiche

MAKE: **10 SERVINGS** HANDS-ON: **1 HOUR 5 MIN.** TOTAL: **3 HOURS 45 MIN.**

6   thick bacon slices
2 ¼   cups milk
2   Tbsp. butter
½   cup uncooked stone-ground grits
2   tsp. kosher salt, divided
1   tsp. black pepper, divided

2 ½   cups shredded sharp Cheddar cheese, divided
6   large eggs, divided
2 ½   cups half-and-half
1   cup heavy cream
⅓   cup sliced green onions
Garnish: chopped fresh chives

1. Preheat oven to 350°. Cook bacon in a skillet over medium heat until crisp. Remove bacon; drain and crumble. Transfer 2 tsp. bacon drippings to a saucepan.

2. Bring drippings, milk, and butter to a boil over medium heat. Gradually whisk in grits, 1 tsp. salt, and ½ tsp. pepper; cook, whisking constantly, 15 minutes or until very thick. Remove from heat; let stand 10 minutes. Stir in 1 cup cheese; let stand 10 minutes. Grease a 9-inch springform pan with cooking spray. Stir 1 egg into grits mixture; spread in springform pan. Bake at 350° for 25 minutes or until set and browned. Sprinkle remaining 1 ½ cups cheese over warm grits, spreading to edges. Let stand 15 minutes.

3. Reduce oven temperature to 325°. Combine half-and-half, cream, onions, and remaining 5 eggs, 1 tsp. salt, and ½ tsp. pepper. Pour over grits; sprinkle with crumbled bacon. Place pan on an aluminum foil-lined baking sheet. Bake at 325° for 1 hour and 15 minutes or until lightly browned and just set. Let stand 20 minutes. Run a sharp knife around edges of quiche; remove sides of pan. Garnish, if desired.

Spread cheese to the edge of the warm, bacony grits "crust" to prevent any custard from seeping out while the quiche bakes.

Cheese Grits and Roasted Tomatoes

MAKES: **4 SERVINGS** HANDS-ON: **25 MIN.** TOTAL: **1 HOUR 5 MIN., INCLUDING TOMATOES**

½   **cup heavy cream**
2   **Tbsp. unsalted butter**
2   **tsp. kosher salt**
1   **cup uncooked stone-ground yellow grits**
2   **oz. cream cheese**

¼   **cup finely grated extra-sharp Cheddar cheese**
Roasted Tomatoes (recipe below)
**Garnishes: chopped fresh chives, freshly ground
    black pepper**

1. Bring first 3 ingredients and 3 cups water to a boil in a medium saucepan over medium-high heat. Stir in grits, and reduce heat to medium-low. Cover and simmer, stirring occasionally, 15 to 20 minutes or until tender.
2. Fold in both cheeses, stirring until melted; remove from heat. Cover and let stand 5 minutes. Transfer to a serving platter. Top with Roasted Tomatoes. Garnish, if desired.

Note: Add up to ¼ cup water after cooking grits, if desired, for a thinner consistency.

Roasted Tomatoes

*Make a double batch of these, and pair the juicy gems
with a cheese tray, salad, or grilled meat.*

1   **lb. cherry tomatoes, halved**
1   **Tbsp. extra virgin olive oil**
1   **Tbsp. red wine vinegar**

1   **tsp. honey**
¼   **tsp. kosher salt**
¼   **tsp. freshly ground black pepper**

Preheat oven to 400°. Toss together cherry tomatoes, olive oil, vinegar, honey, salt, and pepper in a baking dish. Let stand 10 minutes. Bake 18 minutes or until tender. Makes 4 servings.

Cheesy Grits Soufflé

4	tsp. kosher salt, divided		6	Tbsp. butter
2	cups uncooked regular yellow grits		1	jalapeño pepper, seeded and diced
3	cups milk		1	Tbsp. sugar
1½	cups fresh corn kernels (about 3 ears)		1	tsp. hot sauce
6	large eggs, lightly beaten		½	tsp. freshly ground black pepper
2	cups (8 oz.) shredded sharp Cheddar cheese			

1. Preheat oven to 350°. Generously grease (with butter) a 3-qt. baking dish; freeze 10 minutes.

2. Meanwhile, bring 3 cups water and 1 tsp. salt to a boil in a large saucepan over medium-high heat. Gradually whisk in grits; return to a boil. Reduce heat to medium-low, and cook, whisking often, 2 to 3 minutes or until thickened. Whisk in milk, and cook, stirring constantly, 3 to 4 minutes or until grits are creamy.

3. Remove from heat, and stir in corn, next 7 ingredients, and remaining 3 tsp. salt. Spread mixture in prepared dish. Place on an aluminum foil-lined jelly-roll pan.

4. Bake at 350° for 50 minutes or until puffed, firm around edges, and slightly soft in center. Remove from oven to a wire rack, and cool 5 minutes before serving.

This recipe for Cheesy Grits Soufflé turns a classic Southern dish into a light, fluffy soufflé for the ultimate holiday brunch.

Chicks in a Blanket

*Dough-wrapped chicken-apple sausages are best fresh from the oven,
so bake one batch at a time and serve warm.*

MAKES: 8 TO 10 SERVINGS HANDS-ON: 20 MIN. TOTAL: 40 MIN., INCLUDING MUSTARD SAUCE

1 (8-oz.) can refrigerated crescent rolls
1 (12-oz.) package mini smoked chicken-and-
   apple sausages (24 links)
Parchment paper
1 egg yolk, lightly beaten

1 Tbsp. sesame seeds (optional)
1 Tbsp. poppy seeds (optional)
1 Tbsp. fennel seeds (optional)
Spicy Mustard Sauce (recipe below)

1. Preheat oven to 375°. Unroll crescent rolls; separate into triangles. Cut each triangle into 3 long triangles.
2. Place 1 sausage link on wide end of each triangle; roll up triangles around sausages, starting at wide end. Place, point sides down, on a parchment paper-lined baking sheet.
3. Brush rolls with egg yolk. If desired, stir together sesame seeds and next 2 ingredients, and sprinkle over rolls.
4. Bake at 375° for 14 to 15 minutes or until golden brown. Serve with Spicy Mustard Sauce.

Note: We tested with Aidells Chicken & Apple Sausage Minis.

Spicy Mustard Sauce

Honey mustard gets added zip from crushed red pepper and freshly ground black pepper.

½ cup honey mustard
2 Tbsp. olive oil
1 Tbsp. white wine vinegar

1 tsp. dried crushed red pepper
1 tsp. freshly ground black pepper

Stir together honey mustard, olive oil, vinegar, dried crushed red pepper, and freshly ground black pepper. Serve immediately, or cover and chill up to 12 hours. Makes about ¾ cup.

Blueberry Kolaches

Don't overwork the dough. You can use a cookie scoop for easy portioning in Step 4, if desired.

MAKE AHEAD TIP

Prepare through Step 3; chill 8 to 24 hours. Proceed as directed in Steps 4 and 5.

MAKES: ABOUT 3 DOZEN   HANDS-ON: 45 MIN.   TOTAL: 10 HOURS 10 MIN.

1	(¼-oz.) envelope active dry yeast	2	cups milk
½	cup warm water (100° to 110°)	3	(6-oz.) containers fresh blueberries (about 3 cups)
½	cup butter, softened	⅓	cup blueberry preserves
1⅓	cups sugar	⅓	cup all-purpose flour
2½	tsp. table salt	⅓	cup sugar
2	large eggs	3	Tbsp. cold butter, cut up
8½	cups all-purpose flour		

1. Combine yeast and warm water (100° to 110°) in a bowl; let stand 5 minutes.

2. Beat butter at medium speed with an electric mixer until creamy; gradually add 1⅓ cups sugar and 2½ tsp. salt. Add eggs, 1 at a time, beating just until blended after each addition. Stir in yeast mixture.

3. Add 8½ cups flour to butter mixture alternately with milk, beginning and ending with flour mixture. Beat at low speed just until blended, stopping to scrape bowl as needed. Place dough in a well-greased bowl, turning to grease top. Cover with plastic wrap, and chill 8 to 24 hours.

4. Shape dough into 35 (2-inch) balls (about ¼ cup per ball), using floured hands. Place 1½ inches apart on 2 lightly greased baking sheets. Cover and let rise in a warm place (80° to 85°), free from drafts, 1 hour or until doubled in bulk.

5. Preheat oven to 375°. Stir together blueberries and preserves. Combine ⅓ cup flour and next 2 ingredients with a pastry blender until crumbly. Press thumb into each dough ball, forming an indention; fill each with 1 Tbsp. berry mixture. Sprinkle with flour mixture. Bake 20 to 25 minutes or until golden.

Mango Kolaches: Prepare as directed, substituting 2 cups chopped fresh mango for blueberries and ⅓ cup peach preserves for blueberry preserves.

Maple-Pecan Sticky Buns

Our secret is a low-fat roll mix that creates
extra indulgent—and easy—sticky buns. Mornings just got brighter!

MAKES: 16 ROLLS HANDS-ON: 20 MIN. TOTAL: 1 HOUR 30 MIN., INCLUDING SYRUP AND GLAZE

Sticky Bun Syrup (recipe below)
1   (16-oz.) package hot roll mix
3   Tbsp. butter, melted
½   cup firmly packed dark brown sugar

1   tsp. ground cinnamon
Maple Glaze (recipe below)
½   cup chopped toasted pecans

1. Lightly grease 2 (8-inch) round or square cake pans or skillets. Spoon Sticky Bun Syrup into pans.
2. Prepare hot roll dough as directed on back of package; let dough stand 5 minutes.
3. Roll dough into an 18- x 10-inch rectangle. Spread with melted butter. Stir together brown sugar and cinnamon; sprinkle over butter.
4. Roll dough up tightly, starting at 1 long end; cut into 16 slices using a serrated knife. Place 1 slice in center of each prepared pan. Place 7 slices around center roll in each pan.
5. Cover pans loosely with plastic wrap; let rise in a warm place (80° to 85°), free from drafts, 30 to 45 minutes or until doubled in bulk.
6. Preheat oven to 350°. Uncover rolls, and bake 15 to 20 minutes or until golden brown and done. Cool in pans on a wire rack 5 minutes. Prepare Maple Glaze, and brush over rolls. Top with toasted pecans.

Apple-Cinnamon Sticky Rolls: Peel and chop 2 Granny Smith apples (about 3 cups chopped). Place apples in a small microwave-safe bowl, and pour 1 cup apple juice over apples. Cover tightly with heavy-duty plastic wrap; fold back a small corner to allow steam to escape. Microwave at HIGH 5 minutes or until tender. Drain and cool 15 minutes. Prepare recipe as directed, sprinkling apples over brown sugar mixture before rolling up.

Sticky Bun Syrup

This gooey syrup coats the bottom of our Maple-Pecan Sticky Buns, making them extra indulgent.

⅔   cup powdered sugar
¼   cup butter, melted

2   Tbsp. maple syrup
1   egg white

Whisk together powdered sugar, melted butter, maple syrup, and egg white until smooth. Makes about 1 cup.

Maple Glaze

3   Tbsp. butter
¼   cup firmly packed dark brown sugar
2   Tbsp. maple syrup

Pinch of table salt
3   Tbsp. milk

Melt butter in a small, heavy saucepan over medium heat. Whisk in brown sugar, maple syrup, and a pinch of salt until blended. Whisk in milk; bring mixture to a boil, whisking constantly. Reduce heat to medium-low; simmer, whisking constantly, 3 to 4 minutes or until glaze is golden brown and glossy. Use immediately. Makes about ⅔ cup.

Breakfast Bread Dough

This dough does double-duty as Caramel-Glazed Monkey Bread (recipe on page 185) or Chocolate Rolls (recipe below). It's a cinch to mix together and keeps beautifully in the fridge up to 3 days.

MAKE AHEAD TIP

This recipe can be prepared up to 3 days in advance. Store in the refrigerator until ready to use.

MAKES: 1 DOUGH PORTION HANDS-ON: 20 MIN. TOTAL: 2 HOURS 25 MIN.

½ cup warm water (100° to 110°)	1½ tsp. table salt
1 (¼-oz.) envelope active dry yeast	1 tsp. baking soda
1 tsp. sugar	½ cup cold butter, cubed
5 cups all-purpose flour	½ cup shortening, cubed
3 Tbsp. sugar	2 cups buttermilk, at room temperature
5 tsp. baking powder	

1. Stir together first 3 ingredients in a 1-cup glass measuring cup; let stand 5 minutes.
2. Stir together flour and next 4 ingredients in a large bowl; cut butter and shortening into flour mixture with a pastry blender or 2 forks until crumbly. Add yeast mixture and buttermilk, stirring just until dry ingredients are moistened. Cover with plastic wrap, and chill 2 to 72 hours.

Chocolate Rolls

Be sure to use softened butter for spreading to keep the tender dough from tearing.

MAKE AHEAD TIP

Prepare recipe through Step 3. Cover and chill 8 to 24 hours. Let stand 1 hour and 30 minutes. Proceed with Step 5.

MAKES: 16 ROLLS HANDS-ON: 20 MIN.
TOTAL: 4 HOURS 25 MIN., INCLUDING BREAD DOUGH AND GLAZE

Breakfast Bread Dough (recipe above)	2 tsp. ground cinnamon
½ cup butter, softened	2 (4-oz.) bittersweet chocolate baking bars, chopped
⅓ cup granulated sugar	
⅓ cup firmly packed light brown sugar	Vanilla-Orange Glaze (recipe below)

1. Turn Breakfast Bread Dough out onto a lightly floured surface, and knead 3 or 4 times. Roll into a 20- x 14-inch rectangle. Spread with softened butter, leaving a 1-inch border on all sides.
2. Stir together granulated sugar and next 2 ingredients. Sprinkle sugar mixture over butter. Sprinkle chocolate over sugar.
3. Roll dough up tightly, starting at 1 long side; cut into 16 slices using a serrated knife. Place rolls, cut sides down, in a lightly greased 13- x 9-inch pan.
4. Cover and let stand 1 hour.
5. Preheat oven to 350°. Uncover rolls, and bake 25 to 30 minutes or until golden brown. Cool in pan on a wire rack 10 minutes. Drizzle rolls with Vanilla-Orange Glaze, and serve immediately.

Vanilla-Orange Glaze

Orange zest is stirred into this glaze, which is drizzled over our yummy Chocolate Rolls.

2 cups powdered sugar	1 tsp. vanilla extract
3 Tbsp. milk, divided	1 tsp. loosely packed orange zest

Stir together powdered sugar, 2 Tbsp. milk, vanilla, and orange zest. Stir in up to 1 Tbsp. more milk, 1 tsp. at a time, until mixture reaches desired consistency. Makes about 1 cup.

Chocolate Rolls

Caramel-Glazed Monkey Bread

We'd wager our presents under the tree that this is the best pull-apart bread on Earth. The dough is soft and cakey, and the loaf dons a scrumptious sugary crust.

MAKES: 10 TO 12 SERVINGS HANDS-ON: 30 MIN.
TOTAL: 5 HOURS 5 MIN., INCLUDING BREAD DOUGH AND GLAZE

Wax paper
¾ cup granulated sugar
¾ cup firmly packed light brown sugar
1 Tbsp. ground cinnamon

Breakfast Bread Dough (recipe on page 182)
¾ cup butter, melted
1 cup chopped toasted pecans
Caramel Glaze (recipe below)

MAKE AHEAD TIP

Prepare recipe through Step 3. Cover and chill up to 24 hours. Let stand 1 hour and 30 minutes. Proceed as directed in Step 5.

1. Generously grease a 10-inch (12-cup) tube pan; line bottom with wax paper, and lightly grease wax paper.
2. Stir together granulated sugar and next 2 ingredients in a small bowl. Turn Breakfast Bread Dough out onto a lightly floured surface, and knead 3 or 4 times. Shape dough into about 60 (1 ½-inch) balls. Dip each in melted butter; roll in sugar mixture.
3. Place a single layer of coated balls in prepared pan, covering bottom completely. Sprinkle with ⅓ cup pecans. Repeat layers twice. Top with any remaining sugar mixture; drizzle with any remaining melted butter.
4. Cover dough and let stand 1 hour.
5. Preheat oven to 350°. Uncover and bake 40 to 45 minutes or until a wooden pick inserted in center comes out clean. Transfer to a wire rack, and cool 20 minutes. Remove from pan to wire rack, discarding wax paper. Invert onto a serving platter. Drizzle with Caramel Glaze. Serve warm.

Caramel Glaze

This glaze is super easy to prepare and delicious drizzled over Caramel-Glazed Monkey Bread.

¾ cup firmly packed light brown sugar
6 Tbsp. butter

3 Tbsp. milk
1 tsp. vanilla extract

Bring first 3 ingredients to a boil in a small saucepan over medium heat, stirring constantly; boil, stirring constantly, 1 minute. Remove from heat, and stir in vanilla. Stir constantly 2 minutes; use immediately. Makes about ¾ cup.

Ham-and-Swiss Sticky Buns

Stuff the dough deep into the muffin cups so that the tops rise into a cheesy dome while baking.

MAKE AHEAD TIP

Prepare recipe through Step 2, and chill 8 hours. Let stand 10 minutes. Proceed as directed in Step 3.

MAKES: 16 ROLLS HANDS-ON: 20 MIN. TOTAL: 1 HOUR 10 MIN.

9 oz. deli ham, finely chopped	½ cup firmly packed light brown sugar
2 cups (8 oz.) shredded Swiss cheese	2 (16.3-oz.) cans refrigerated jumbo biscuits
2 Tbsp. spicy brown mustard	Maple syrup

1. Preheat oven to 325°. Stir together first 3 ingredients.

2. Sprinkle brown sugar into a 12-inch square on a clean surface. Arrange biscuits in 4 rows on sugar, covering sugar completely. Pinch biscuits together to form a square. Roll dough to a 16- x 12-inch rectangle (about ¼ inch thick), pinching dough together as needed. Spread ham-and-cheese mixture over dough. Roll up tightly, starting at 1 long side, pressing brown sugar into dough as you roll. Pinch ends to seal. Cut into 16 slices using a serrated knife. Fit each slice into cups of a lightly greased 24-cup muffin pan. (Dough will extend over tops of cups.)

3. Bake at 325° for 40 minutes or until golden and centers are completely cooked. Cool on a wire rack 10 minutes. Drizzle with syrup.

Note: We tested with Pillsbury Grands! Flaky Layers Original refrigerated biscuits.

Christmas Morning Sticky Buns

MAKES: 8 SERVINGS HANDS-ON: 25 MIN. TOTAL: 8 HOURS 55 MIN.

½ cup chopped pecans or walnuts	½ cup butter, melted
1 (25-oz.) package frozen roll dough, thawed	½ cup firmly packed brown sugar
1 (3.4-oz.) package butterscotch instant pudding mix	¾ tsp. ground cinnamon

1. Sprinkle pecans in the bottom of a greased (with butter) 12-cup Bundt pan. Arrange dough in pan; sprinkle with dry pudding mix.

2. Stir together butter, brown sugar, and cinnamon; pour over rolls. Cover and chill 8 hours.

3. Preheat oven to 350°. Bake for 30 minutes or until golden brown. Invert onto a serving plate, and serve immediately.

Ham-and-Swiss
Sticky Buns

Banana Foster Coffee Cake with Vanilla Rum Sauce

MAKES: **8 TO 10 SERVINGS** HANDS-ON: **20 MIN.** TOTAL: **1 HOUR 45 MIN.**

1½ cups mashed ripe bananas

7 Tbsp. light rum, divided

2 cups firmly packed brown sugar, divided

1½ cups butter, softened and divided

2 tsp. vanilla extract, divided

8 oz. cream cheese, softened

2 large eggs

3¼ cups plus 3 Tbsp. all-purpose flour, divided

⅝ tsp. table salt, divided

½ tsp. baking powder

½ tsp. baking soda

1½ cups chopped pecans

1 tsp. ground cinnamon

1 cup granulated sugar

2 cups heavy cream

1. Preheat oven to 350°. Cook bananas, 3 Tbsp. rum, ½ cup brown sugar, and ¼ cup butter in a skillet until mixture is bubbly. Cool; stir in 1 tsp. vanilla.

2. Beat cream cheese and ½ cup butter at medium speed with an electric mixer until creamy. Add 1 cup brown sugar; beat until fluffy. Beat in eggs 1 at a time.

3. Stir together 3 cups flour, ½ tsp. salt, and next 2 ingredients; add to cream cheese mixture. Beat at low speed to blend. Stir in banana mixture. Spoon into a greased and floured 13- x 9-inch pan.

4. Combine pecans, cinnamon, ½ cup brown sugar, and ¼ cup flour. Melt ¼ cup butter; stir into pecan mixture. Sprinkle over batter. Bake at 350° for 45 minutes or until a wooden pick inserted in center comes out clean. Cool in pan on a wire rack 10 minutes.

5. Combine granulated sugar, 3 Tbsp. flour, and ⅛ tsp. salt in a saucepan over medium heat. Add cream and ½ cup butter; bring to a boil. Boil, whisking constantly, 2 minutes or until slightly thickened. Remove from heat; stir in ¼ cup rum and 1 tsp. vanilla. Drizzle sauce over cake.

Substitute extra cream for rum in the sauce, if you prefer.

Chocolate Breakfast Wreath

Be sure to soften butter until it's spreadable. The silky dough is a dream to work with, so even beginning bakers can make this beautiful wreath. Try this chocolate version or Citrus-Cranberry.

MAKES: **8 SERVINGS** HANDS-ON: **45 MIN.** TOTAL: **4 HOURS, INCLUDING GLAZE**

½ cup warm milk (100°)
2 (¼-oz.) envelopes active dry yeast
⅓ cup plus ½ cup sugar, divided
4 ½ cups all-purpose flour, divided
2 tsp. kosher salt
1 ½ cups butter, softened and divided

3 large eggs, at room temperature
Parchment paper
1 (4-oz.) bittersweet chocolate baking bar, finely chopped
Easy Vanilla Glaze (recipe below)

1. Combine milk, yeast, and ⅓ cup sugar in bowl of a heavy-duty electric stand mixer; let stand 5 minutes or until foamy. Gradually add 1 cup flour, beating at low speed until blended; scrape down sides. Add salt and 1 cup butter; beat at low speed until smooth. Add eggs, 1 at a time, beating until incorporated after each addition and scraping sides of bowl as needed. Gradually add remaining 3 ½ cups flour, beating until blended. Increase speed to medium, and beat until dough forms a ball and begins to pull away from sides. Beat dough 2 more minutes or until smooth and elastic. Turn dough out onto a lightly floured surface, and knead 3 minutes.

2. Place dough in a large greased bowl, turning to grease top. Cover with plastic wrap, and let rise in a warm place (80° to 85°), free from drafts, 1 hour or until doubled in bulk. Punch dough down, and turn out onto lightly floured parchment paper. Roll dough into an 18- x 12-inch rectangle.

3. Brush 6 Tbsp. softened butter over dough; sprinkle with chocolate and ½ cup sugar. Roll up dough, jelly-roll fashion, starting at 1 long side. Press edge to seal, and place dough, seam side down, on parchment paper.

4. Transfer parchment paper with dough onto a baking sheet. Shape rolled dough into a ring, pressing ends together to seal. Cut ring at 2-inch intervals, from outer edge up to (but not through) inside edge. Gently pull and twist cut pieces to show filling. Cover dough.

5. Let rise in a warm place (80° to 85°), free from drafts, 1 hour or until doubled in bulk. Preheat oven to 350°. Uncover dough. Melt remaining 2 Tbsp. butter; brush over dough. Bake 30 to 40 minutes or until golden. Cool on baking sheet 10 minutes. Drizzle Easy Vanilla Glaze over warm bread.

Citrus-Cranberry Wreath: Omit chocolate and Easy Vanilla Glaze. Soak 1 cup sweetened dried cranberries in 1 cup boiling water 15 minutes; drain and pat cranberries dry. Prepare breakfast wreath recipe as directed through step 3, sprinkling cranberries over dough and 1 Tbsp. loosely packed orange zest over cranberries before rolling. Proceed as directed in steps 4 and 5. Beat together 3 oz. softened cream cheese and 1 Tbsp. softened butter in a medium bowl at medium speed with an electric mixer. Gradually add 2 cups powdered sugar to cream cheese mixture alternately with 2 Tbsp. fresh orange juice, beating at medium speed after each addition. Add up to 2 Tbsp. fresh orange juice, 1 tsp. at a time, until desired consistency is reached. Drizzle over bread.

Easy Vanilla Glaze

Whisk together 2 cups powdered sugar, 3 Tbsp. milk, ½ tsp. vanilla extract, and a dash of table salt. Whisk in up to 1 Tbsp. milk, 1 tsp. at a time, until desired consistency is reached. Makes 1 ½ cups.

New Orleans Calas

The Calas Women, as they were called, peddled these hot breakfast fritters—whose name comes from the African word "kárá"—each morning in the French Quarter. The street vendors have vanished, so we honor them here with a classic rice-dough recipe too delicious to ever disappear.

MAKES: ABOUT 2 ½ DOZEN HANDS-ON: 45 MIN. TOTAL: 10 HOURS 10 MIN.

½   cup uncooked medium-grain rice
¾   tsp. table salt, divided
½   cup warm water (100° to 110°)
1 ¼ tsp. active dry yeast
1   tsp. granulated sugar
3   large eggs, lightly beaten

1 ¼ cups all-purpose flour
¼   cup granulated sugar
¼   tsp. ground nutmeg
Vegetable oil
Powdered sugar

1. Bring 6 cups water to a boil in a saucepan over medium-high heat. Stir in rice and ¼ tsp. salt. Reduce heat to medium, and cook, stirring often, 25 to 30 minutes. (Rice will be very soft and thick.) Remove from heat, and drain. Place 1 ½ cups cooked rice in a bowl, discarding remaining rice. Mash rice with a potato masher 30 seconds. Cool 20 minutes or until lukewarm.

2. Stir together warm water (100° to 110°), yeast, and 1 tsp. granulated sugar in a 1-cup glass measuring cup; let stand 5 minutes. Stir yeast mixture into rice. Cover with plastic wrap, and let stand in a warm place (80° to 85°), free from drafts, 8 to 12 hours.

3. Stir eggs into rice mixture. Combine flour, next 2 ingredients, and remaining ½ tsp. salt. Stir flour mixture into rice mixture. Cover with plastic wrap, and let stand in a warm place (80° to 85°), free from drafts, 30 minutes.

4. Meanwhile, pour oil to depth of 3 inches into a deep cast-iron skillet or large Dutch oven; heat to 350°. Drop dough by rounded tablespoonfuls into the hot oil, and fry, in batches, 3 minutes or until golden brown. Drain on paper towels. Sprinkle with powdered sugar, and serve immediately.

Note: We tested with Water Maid Medium-Grain Enriched Rice.

Gluten-Free Buttermilk Pecan-Walnut Cake

MAKES: **10 TO 12 SERVINGS** HANDS-ON: **45 MIN.**
TOTAL: **2 HOURS 5 MIN., INCLUDING COFFEE CREAM**

6	Tbsp. turbinado sugar, divided	6	large eggs
4	cups pecan halves, toasted	¾	cup buttermilk
3	cups walnut halves, toasted	½	cup half-and-half
1½	cups slivered almonds, toasted	1	tsp. kosher salt
¾	cup finely ground plain white cornmeal	1	tsp. vanilla extract
1	cup butter, softened		Coffee Cream (recipe below)
¾	cup firmly packed light brown sugar		

1. Preheat oven to 350°. Sprinkle 3 Tbsp. turbinado sugar in a well-greased (with butter) 12-inch cast-iron skillet. Process pecans, walnuts, and almonds in a food processor until coarsely chopped; reserve 2 cups coarsely chopped nuts. Add cornmeal to remaining nuts in processor; pulse until nuts are finely chopped.
2. Beat butter and brown sugar at medium speed with an electric mixer 2 to 3 minutes or until light and fluffy.
3. Whisk together eggs and next 4 ingredients in a medium bowl. Gradually add egg mixture to butter mixture, beating at low speed 2 minutes or until blended, stopping to scrape bowl as needed. Gradually add cornmeal mixture to batter, beating until well blended; fold in reserved 2 cups coarsely chopped nuts. Spoon batter into prepared skillet. Level batter using an offset spatula, and sprinkle remaining 3 Tbsp. turbinado sugar over batter.
4. Bake at 350° for 45 to 55 minutes or until a wooden pick inserted in center comes out clean. Cool completely on a wire rack. Serve with Coffee Cream.

Coffee Cream

Stir together 1 cup heavy cream and ½ tsp. instant dark roast coffee or instant espresso in a medium bowl until well blended. Beat at high speed with an electric mixer 1 minute. Gradually add 6 Tbsp. powdered sugar, beating until soft peaks form. Makes 2½ cups.

Cranberry-Orange Muffins

Sprinkle the tops of the glazed muffins with coarse sugar to add texture and a little sparkle.

MAKES: 2 DOZEN HANDS-ON: 45 MIN. TOTAL: 1 HOUR 20 MIN.

¾ cup butter, softened
2 ⅓ cups granulated sugar, divided
4 large eggs
2 Tbsp. loosely packed orange zest
2 ½ cups plus 1 Tbsp. all-purpose flour
½ cup plain yellow cornmeal
2 tsp. baking powder

½ tsp. table salt
1 cup milk
2 cups fresh cranberries, coarsely chopped
4 ½ tsp. fresh orange juice
4 ½ tsp. fresh lemon juice
Turbinado sugar (optional)

1. Preheat oven to 350°. Beat butter with an electric mixer until creamy; gradually add 2 cups granulated sugar, beating until light and fluffy. Add eggs, 1 at a time, beating until blended after each addition. Beat in zest.

2. Stir together 2 ½ cups flour and next 3 ingredients; add to butter mixture alternately with milk, beginning and ending with flour mixture. Toss cranberries with 1 Tbsp. flour. Fold cranberries into batter. Grease 2 (12-cup) muffin pans with cooking spray. Divide batter evenly between muffin pans.

3. Bake at 350° for 25 minutes or until a wooden pick inserted in center comes out clean. Meanwhile, bring orange juice, lemon juice, and remaining ⅓ cup granulated sugar to a boil in a small saucepan over medium heat. Boil until sugar is completely dissolved and syrup has thickened slightly (about 1 minute).

4. Pierce top of each muffin several times with a wooden pick, and brush warm syrup mixture over muffins. Sprinkle tops of muffins with turbinado sugar, if desired. Cool in pans on wire racks 10 minutes.

Blueberry-Lemon Muffins: Omit orange juice. Prepare recipe as directed, substituting lemon zest for orange zest and fresh whole blueberries or frozen blueberries for cranberries. (Do not chop blueberries.) Increase lemon juice to 3 Tbsp. Bake at 350° for 25 minutes or until a wooden pick inserted in center comes out clean.

Brown Sugar-Toasted Pecan Muffins: Omit cranberries and 1 Tbsp. flour. Prepare recipe as directed, substituting light brown sugar for granulated sugar and adding 1 tsp. vanilla extract with orange zest at end of Step 1. Stir 2 cups chopped, toasted pecans into batter. Bake at 350° for 18 to 22 minutes.

Gingerbread Muffins

We know, serving streusel-topped muffins with hard sauce
is gilding the lily, but hey, it's Christmas morning after all.

MAKES: 1 ½ DOZEN HANDS-ON: 30 MIN.
TOTAL: 1 HOUR 45 MIN., INCLUDING STREUSEL AND SAUCE

2 ½ cups all-purpose flour	½ cup firmly packed light brown sugar
⅓ cup chopped crystallized ginger	2 large eggs
1 tsp. baking soda	¾ cup hot brewed coffee
½ tsp. table salt	⅔ cup molasses
½ tsp. ground cinnamon	18 paper baking cups
⅛ tsp. ground cloves	Spiced Streusel (recipe below)
¾ cup butter, softened	Spiced Hard Sauce (recipe below)
½ cup granulated sugar	

1. Preheat oven to 350°. Process first 6 ingredients in a food processor 1 minute or until ginger is finely chopped.

2. Beat butter at medium speed with a heavy-duty electric stand mixer until creamy. Gradually add both sugars, beating until light and fluffy. Add eggs, 1 at a time, beating just until blended after each addition.

3. Stir together hot coffee and molasses in a small bowl. Add flour mixture to butter mixture alternately with coffee mixture, beginning and ending with flour mixture. Beat at low speed just until blended after each addition.

4. Place baking cups in 2 (12-cup) muffin pans, and lightly grease; spoon batter into cups, filling two-thirds full. Sprinkle with Spiced Streusel.

5. Bake at 350° for 18 to 20 minutes or until a wooden pick inserted in center comes out clean. Cool in pans on wire racks 5 minutes. Remove from pans to wire racks, and cool completely (about 30 minutes). Top with Spiced Hard Sauce.

Spiced Streusel

Spiced Streusel is the perfect crunchy finale to our Gingerbread Muffins.

MAKE AHEAD TIP

Chill in an airtight container for up to 1 week.

½ cup firmly packed light brown sugar	¼ tsp. ground nutmeg
2 Tbsp. all-purpose flour	1 cup chopped pecans
1 ½ tsp. ground cinnamon	2 Tbsp. butter, melted
¼ tsp. ground cloves	

Stir together brown sugar, flour, cinnamon, cloves, and nutmeg; stir in chopped pecans and melted butter until crumbly. Makes about 1 ½ cups.

Spiced Hard Sauce

Add extra decadence to Gingerbread Muffins by topping with Spiced Hard Sauce.

MAKE AHEAD TIP

Chill as above. Let stand 20 minutes before using.

1 cup butter, softened	¼ tsp. ground nutmeg
2 Tbsp. milk	3 cups powdered sugar
¼ tsp. ground cinnamon	2 tsp. vanilla extract

Beat butter, milk, cinnamon, and nutmeg at medium speed with an electric mixer until creamy. Gradually add powdered sugar and vanilla, beating until light and fluffy. Makes about 2 cups.

Ambrosia with Chantilly Cream

The original ambrosia recipe is simply a layering of orange slices, sugar, and toasted unsweetened coconut. Over the years, folks began to add pineapple, maraschino cherries, and whipped cream to create more of a fruit salad, but the name stuck.

MAKES: 8 TO 10 SERVINGS HANDS-ON: 50 MIN.
TOTAL: 9 HOURS 10 MIN., INCLUDING CHANTILLY CREAM

MAKE AHEAD TIP

1	cup sugar
¾	cup fresh mint, divided
3	navel oranges, peeled and sectioned
3	blood oranges, peeled and sectioned
2	grapefruit, peeled and sectioned
6	clementines, peeled and sectioned
	Chantilly Cream
	Garnish: fresh mint leaves

Steep fresh mint in hot sugar syrup to make a tasty simple syrup up to a week in advance. Section the citrus, and toss it with syrup the day before.

1. Bring sugar and ½ cup water to a boil; stir until sugar dissolves. Boil 5 minutes. Remove from heat; steep ½ cup mint 20 minutes. Strain syrup; discard solids. Cool syrup completely.

2. Toss together citrus sections and ¼ cup syrup. Cover and chill 8 hours, stirring occasionally. (Reserve remaining syrup for another use.) Chop remaining ¼ cup mint; toss with fruit. Serve with Chantilly Cream.

Chantilly Cream

1	(8-oz.) container crème fraîche or sour cream
¾	cup whipping cream
¾	tsp. vanilla extract
3	Tbsp. powdered sugar

Beat crème fraîche in a large bowl at medium speed with an electric mixer 30 seconds. Add remaining ingredients; beat at high speed 3 minutes or until soft peaks form. Makes about 2 ½ cups.

SECOND HELPINGS

Rethink your leftovers and unused ingredients.
We upgraded the iconic day-after sandwich
with some fresh alternatives

New Turkey Tetrazzini

Loads of spinach and mushrooms freshen up this classic.

MAKES: 8 TO 10 SERVINGS HANDS-ON: 50 MIN. TOTAL: 1 HOUR 15 MIN.

12	oz. uncooked rotini pasta	2	cups stuffing mix, divided
1	(8-oz.) package fresh cremini mushrooms, sliced	⅓	cup all-purpose flour
5	Tbsp. butter, divided	2½	cups milk
2	cups diced yellow onion	2½	cups reduced-sodium chicken broth
3	garlic cloves, minced	½	tsp. table salt
½	cup dry white wine	½	tsp. black pepper
1	(12-oz.) package fresh baby spinach	2	(5-oz.) packages buttery garlic-and-herb spreadable cheese
3	cups shredded cooked turkey		

1. Preheat oven to 350°. Cook pasta according to package directions. Meanwhile, sauté mushrooms 4 minutes in 2 Tbsp. melted butter in a large skillet over medium-high heat. Add onions and garlic; sauté 3 minutes. Stir in wine, and cook 4 minutes or until liquid almost evaporates. Add half of spinach, and cook, stirring constantly, until wilted; repeat with remaining spinach. Stir together shredded turkey, mushroom mixture, cooked pasta, and 1 cup stuffing mix in a large bowl.

2. Heat remaining 3 Tbsp. butter in a large saucepan over medium heat until foamy. Whisk in flour, and cook, whisking occasionally, 3 minutes. Whisk in milk and chicken broth, stirring until combined and smooth. Increase heat to medium-high, and cook, whisking often, 10 minutes or until mixture begins to bubble. (Do not boil.) Whisk in salt, pepper, and 1 package garlic-and-herb cheese; simmer, whisking often, 4 minutes or until thickened. Add milk mixture to pasta mixture; stir until well blended. Spoon mixture into a well-greased (with butter) 9- x 13-inch baking dish. Dot with remaining package garlic-and-herb cheese; sprinkle with remaining 1 cup stuffing mix.

3. Bake at 350° for 20 to 30 minutes or until browned and bubbly. Cool 5 to 10 minutes before serving.

Note: We tested with Boursin Garlic & Fine Herbs Gournay Cheese and Stove Top Stuffing Mix for Turkey.

Green Bean Quiche

*What's better than a clever new guise for leftover green bean casserole
(onion topping and all)? This one takes just 5 minutes to mix.*

MAKES: 8 TO 10 SERVINGS   HANDS-ON: 5 MIN.   TOTAL: 1 HOUR

2	cups (8 oz.) shredded Swiss cheese	¼	cup butter, melted
1	cup grated Parmesan	4	large eggs
¾	cup all-purpose baking mix	2	cups leftover green bean casserole
½	tsp. table salt	⅓	cup sliced almonds
2	cups 1% low-fat milk		

Preheat oven to 350°. Combine first 7 ingredients; fold in casserole. Spoon into a greased (with butter) 10-inch pie plate. Top with almonds. Bake 45 minutes or until set. Cool 10 minutes.

Note: We tested with Bisquick Original Pancake & Baking Mix.

Sausage-and-Sweet Potato Soup

*A smart way to repurpose sweet potato casserole, this hearty soup drew rave reviews
in our Test Kitchen. If your casserole contains marshmallows, remove them
before stirring the casserole into this soup. The flavor will vary depending on your
casserole recipe; simply adjust salt and pepper to taste before serving.*

MAKES: ABOUT 2 QT.   HANDS-ON: 30 MIN.   TOTAL: 55 MIN.

1	lb. smoked sausage, sliced	1	medium-size red bell pepper, chopped
1	medium-size yellow onion, thinly sliced	1	tsp. fresh thyme leaves
3	garlic cloves, sliced	1	(5-oz.) package baby kale leaves
6	cups reduced-sodium chicken broth		or spinach
2	cups leftover sweet potato casserole (without marshmallow topping)		Multigrain crackers

1. Cook sausage in a Dutch oven over medium heat, stirring occasionally, 7 to 8 minutes or until browned. Remove sausage from Dutch oven, using a slotted spoon. Reserve 2 Tbsp. drippings in Dutch oven.
2. Sauté onion in hot drippings in Dutch oven over medium-high heat 5 to 6 minutes or until tender. Add garlic, and sauté 2 minutes. Add broth, next 3 ingredients, and cooked sausage; bring to a boil. Reduce heat to medium, and simmer 20 minutes.
3. Add kale, and simmer 5 minutes. Add salt and pepper to taste. Serve with crackers.

Sausage-and-Sweet Potato Soup

Green Bean Quiche

Lemongrass-Turkey Soup

Sausage-and-Sweet Potato Soup, p. 206

Lemongrass-Turkey Soup

For a heartier spin, serve it over rice or noodles.
Can't find fresh lemongrass in the produce section of your supermarket?
Try our version that uses Thai ginger-infused chicken broth instead.

MAKES: 2 QT. HANDS-ON: 20 MIN. TOTAL: 1 HOUR

1 (6-inch) lemongrass stalk	½ (8-oz.) package fresh button mushrooms, sliced
6 cups reduced-sodium chicken broth	1 jalapeño pepper, thinly sliced (optional)
6 garlic cloves	Toppings: hot sauce, sliced green onions, chopped fresh cilantro
1 Tbsp. grated fresh ginger	
2 cups shredded cooked turkey or chicken	
1½ cups sliced snow peas	

1. Trim and discard root end and tough outer leaves of lemongrass stalk; smash with flat side of knife.

2. Bring broth, garlic, ginger, and lemongrass to a boil in a covered Dutch oven over high heat. Reduce heat to medium; simmer 20 minutes. Remove from heat; let stand to infuse 15 minutes. Discard lemongrass and garlic.

3. Bring broth mixture to a boil over medium-high heat; stir in turkey, next 2 ingredients, and, if desired, jalapeño. Boil 3 minutes. Serve with toppings.

Speedy Lemongrass-Turkey Soup: Omit lemongrass, garlic, and ginger; substitute 1 (32-oz.) container Thai ginger-infused broth for reduced-sodium chicken broth. Omit Steps 1 and 2; prepare recipe as directed in Step 3.

Black-Eyed Peas, Collard, and Sweet Potato Stew

Don't be intimidated by the length of the ingredient list for this thrifty Southern stew. The majority of the ingredients are used to make a fantastic stock that starts with a Southern classic: potlikker. Then we use loads of fresh, aromatic vegetables, herbs, and spices to round out the flavor. Serve the stew ladled over hot cooked rice, and sprinkle with fresh herbs.

MAKES: 1 ½ QT. HANDS-ON: 1 HOUR 30 MIN. TOTAL: 4 HOURS 20 MIN.

1 bunch fresh collard greens (1 lb.)	¼ cup sugar
6 whole cloves	5 Tbsp. rice vinegar
1 medium-size yellow onion, halved	¼ cup soy sauce
2 Tbsp. vegetable oil	2 smoked ham hocks
10 fresh parsley stems	1 lb. chicken wings
10 fresh cilantro stems	1 lb. pork neck bones
4 fresh thyme sprigs	1 (16-oz.) package dried black-eyed peas
4 celery ribs, peeled and coarsely chopped	2 medium-size sweet potatoes, peeled and cubed
3 bay leaves	
3 large carrots, peeled and coarsely chopped	2 tsp. kosher salt
1 garlic bulb, halved	Freshly ground black pepper
2 (2-inch) pieces fresh ginger, peeled and crushed	Hot sauce
	6 cups hot cooked rice
1 (14.5-oz.) can diced tomatoes, drained	
1 tsp. dried crushed red pepper	

1. Remove and chop collard stems. Chop collard leaves. Insert 3 whole cloves in each onion half, and place onions, cut sides down, in hot oil in a Dutch oven over medium-high heat. Add parsley stems, next 9 ingredients, and collard stems. Cook, stirring gently, 10 minutes or until vegetables begin to soften. Add 4 qt. water, and whisk in sugar, rice vinegar, and soy sauce; cook 1 minute, stirring to blend. Add ham hocks, chicken wings, and pork neck bones. Bring to a boil, skimming off foam. Reduce heat to low; simmer 3 hours or until ham hocks are tender and potlikker is rich in flavor, skimming as necessary.

2. Meanwhile, rinse and sort peas. Bring peas and water to cover to a boil in a large saucepan over high heat. Cook 2 minutes, skimming off foam. Drain peas.

3. Pour potlikker through a fine wire-mesh strainer into an 8-cup glass measuring cup, reserving hocks, chicken wings, and pork neck bones; discard remaining solids. Remove and chop meat from ham hocks, chicken wings, and pork neck bones; discard bones and skin.

4. Wipe Dutch oven clean, and return potlikker to Dutch oven. Add drained peas, chopped ham, chicken, pork, and collard leaves to potlikker. Bring to a boil over high heat, reduce heat to medium-low, and simmer, stirring occasionally, 15 minutes or until peas are just tender. Stir in sweet potatoes, and cook, stirring occasionally, 10 minutes or until peas and sweet potatoes are tender. Stir in 2 tsp. kosher salt. Add freshly ground black pepper and hot sauce to taste. Adjust seasoning, if desired. Serve stew over hot cooked rice. Serve with hot sauce, if desired.

Curried Chicken Chowder

MAKES: **ABOUT 16 CUPS** HANDS-ON: **40 MIN.** TOTAL: **1 HOUR**

2 cups diced sweet onion (about 1 large)
1 cup diced celery
1 cup diced carrots
2 Tbsp. canola oil
2 garlic cloves, minced
6 cups chicken broth
1 lb. Yukon gold potatoes, peeled and cubed
1 lb. sweet potatoes, peeled and cubed
4 cups shredded cooked chicken

3 cups fresh yellow corn kernels (about 6 ears)
2 cups uncooked, shelled frozen edamame (green soybeans)
1 (13.5-oz.) can unsweetened coconut milk
1 Tbsp. curry powder
2 tsp. table salt
1 tsp. freshly ground black pepper
Toppings: toasted coconut, green onions, peanuts, lime wedges

Sauté first 3 ingredients in hot oil in a large Dutch oven or stockpot over medium-high heat 5 minutes or until tender; add garlic, and sauté 1 minute. Add broth and the next 9 ingredients; bring to a boil, stirring often. Reduce heat to medium, and simmer, stirring occasionally, 20 to 25 minutes or until vegetables are tender. Add salt and pepper to taste. Serve with desired toppings.

To Freeze: To preserve the textures of meat and vegetables in hot soup, it's important to cool hot soups completely before freezing. To quickly reduce the temperature, transfer to a large, shallow container (13- x 9-inch baking dish). Refrigerate uncovered, stirring occasionally, until cool. Transfer to airtight containers or zip-top freezer bags. Freeze up to 1 month. Thaw in refrigerator 8 hours.

Warm up and fill up with a big batch of Curried Chicken Chowder. The coconut milk adds a touch of sweetness to the curried soup.

Twice-Baked Potatoes Four Ways

Pick your favorite filling for these savory delights.

MAKES: 8 POTATOES HANDS-ON: 15 MIN. TOTAL: 1 HOUR 40 MIN.

4   (10- to 12-oz.) russet potatoes
½   (8-oz.) package ⅓-less-fat cream cheese, cubed and softened
½   cup milk

Desired Potato Filling (recipes below):
    Chicken, Broccoli, and Cheddar Potato
    Filling; BBQ Pork and Pepper Jack Potato
    Filling; Caramelized Onion, Bacon, and
    Goat Cheese Potato Filling

1. Preheat oven to 400°. Pierce potatoes several times with a fork, and bake directly on oven rack 1 hour or until potatoes are tender. (Baking directly on the rack keeps skins crisp and firm to hold the filling.) Cool 10 minutes.

2. Lightly grease a baking sheet with cooking spray. Cut potatoes in half lengthwise; carefully scoop pulp into a large bowl, leaving shells intact. Mash together potato pulp, cream cheese, and milk; stir in desired Potato Filling. Spoon mixture into potato shells, and place on baking sheet.

3. Bake at 400° for 15 to 20 minutes or until thoroughly heated.

To Freeze: Prepare through Step 2. Freeze potatoes on a baking sheet 1 hour or until firm. Wrap each potato in plastic wrap, place in a zip-top plastic freezer bag, and freeze up to 1 month. Thaw in refrigerator overnight. To serve, unwrap potatoes, and bake at 350° for 45 minutes or until hot. Or microwave at HIGH 5 minutes or until hot, checking at 1-minute intervals.

Potato Fillings

Chicken, Broccoli, and Cheddar: Melt 2 Tbsp. butter in a large skillet over medium-high heat; add 1 small onion, diced, and 1 (10-oz.) package frozen chopped broccoli, thawed and drained; sauté 5 minutes or until tender. Stir together broccoli mixture, 2 cups chopped cooked chicken, 1 ½ cups (6 oz.) shredded sharp Cheddar cheese, ¾ tsp. table salt, and ½ tsp. freshly ground black pepper. Total time 20 minutes.

BBQ Pork and Pepper Jack: Stir together 2 cups (about ½ lb.) chopped barbecued pork (without sauce), 1 ½ cups (6 oz.) shredded pepper Jack cheese, ⅓ cup minced green onions, and 4 tsp. Ranch dressing mix. Serve potatoes with barbecue sauce. Total time 10 minutes.

Caramelized Onion, Bacon, and Goat Cheese: Melt 2 Tbsp. butter in a large skillet over medium-high heat; add 2 cups chopped red onion and 2 tsp. sugar, and sauté 10 to 12 minutes or until caramelized. Stir in 2 Tbsp. dry sherry, and cook 1 minute or until liquid evaporates, stirring to loosen particles from bottom of skillet. Stir together onion mixture; 1 (4-oz.) goat cheese log, softened; 8 cooked and crumbled bacon slices; 2 Tbsp. chopped fresh thyme; ¾ tsp. table salt; and ½ tsp. ground black pepper. Total time 20 minutes.

Chicken, Broccoli, and Cheddar Twice-Baked Potatoes

Collard Green Carbonara

MAKES: **6 TO 8 SERVINGS** HANDS-ON: **35 MIN.** TOTAL: **35 MIN.**

12   oz. uncooked spaghetti
6   thick hickory-smoked bacon slices, chopped
1   medium-size red onion, halved and sliced
2   garlic cloves, minced
4   cups firmly packed chopped
     fresh collard greens
3   large pasteurized eggs, lightly beaten

1   large pasteurized egg yolk, lightly beaten
1   tsp. kosher salt
1   tsp. ground black pepper
½   tsp. dried crushed red pepper
3   cups (12 oz.) freshly shredded Parmigiano-
     Reggiano cheese, divided

1. Cook pasta according to package directions.

2. Meanwhile, cook bacon in a large skillet over medium-high heat 5 to 6 minutes or until crisp; drain on paper towels, reserving drippings in skillet.

3. Sauté onion in hot drippings 4 to 5 minutes or until golden brown and tender. Add garlic; sauté 1 minute. Add collards; sauté 5 minutes. Remove from heat. Add bacon.

4. Whisk together eggs, egg yolk, next 3 ingredients, and 2 ½ cups cheese in a large bowl. Drain pasta, reserving ½ cup pasta water, and immediately pour hot pasta into egg mixture; toss to coat. (The heat from the pasta will partially cook the eggs.) Add collard mixture; toss to combine. Stir in enough pasta water to reach desired consistency. Sprinkle with remaining ½ cup cheese.

Pasta carbonara is the ultimate quick dinner. It's rich, satisfying, and works during the week but is worthy of weekend company.

Sweet Potato Casserole Hotcakes

MAKES: **ABOUT 18 PANCAKES** HANDS-ON: **30 MIN.** TOTAL: **30 MIN.**

½ cup maple syrup
3 Tbsp. leftover cranberry sauce or whole-berry cranberry sauce
1½ cups milk
1 cup leftover sweet potato casserole
¼ cup butter, melted
2 large eggs

½ tsp. vanilla extract
1¾ cups all-purpose flour
2 Tbsp. light brown sugar
1 Tbsp. baking powder
½ tsp. ground cinnamon
½ tsp. kosher salt

1. Stir together first 2 ingredients.
2. Whisk together milk and next 4 ingredients in a large bowl. Whisk together flour and next 4 ingredients in another bowl. Gradually stir flour mixture into milk mixture just until dry ingredients are moistened.
3. Pour about ¼ cup batter for each pancake onto a hot (about 350°), lightly greased (with butter) griddle or large nonstick skillet. Cook over medium heat 2 to 3 minutes or until tops are covered with bubbles and edges look dry and cooked; turn and cook 1 to 2 more minutes or until puffed and thoroughly cooked. Serve immediately with syrup mixture, or place in a single layer on a baking sheet and keep warm in a 200° oven up to 30 minutes.

If your sweet potato casserole is very sweet, omit the brown sugar in the pancakes. Does yours come with a marshmallow topping? Even better. Simply stir it into your sweet potatoes, and make the recipe as directed.

DECADENT DESSERTS

Satisfy everyone's sweet tooth with these scrumptious recipes. They make a delicious ending to any meal or are just perfect for a holiday gift

Pecan Linzer Cookies

MAKES: **ABOUT 2 DOZEN** HANDS-ON: **1 HOUR** TOTAL: **6 HOURS 10 MIN.**

2 ¼ cups all-purpose flour
1   cup pecan halves
1   tsp. ground cinnamon
½   tsp. ground cloves
1   cup butter, very soft
⅓   cup granulated sugar

1   tsp. loosely packed lemon zest
1   large egg
1   large egg yolk
Parchment paper
¼   cup powdered sugar
¾   cup peach jam

1. Pulse first 4 ingredients in a food processor until finely ground.

2. Beat butter, sugar, and zest at medium speed with an electric mixer 1 minute. Add egg and egg yolk; beat 30 seconds. Scrape bowl; beat 30 seconds. Add flour mixture, beating until combined.

3. Shape dough into 2 (½-inch-thick) rectangles. Wrap each rectangle in plastic wrap, and chill 4 hours to 3 days.

4. Preheat oven to 350°. Generously flour both sides of dough; place on parchment paper. Roll each into a 14- x 10-inch rectangle. Cut each rectangle into 24 (2-inch) squares, rerolling scraps as needed. Chill on parchment paper 30 minutes.

5. Place cookies 1 inch apart on parchment paper-lined baking sheets. Cut centers out of half of cookies with a lightly floured 1 ¼-inch square cutter. (If desired, place dough centers on a parchment paper-lined baking sheet; chill 15 minutes, and bake as directed.)

6. Bake at 350° for 12 to 14 minutes or until edges are golden. Cool completely on parchment paper on a wire rack. Repeat with remaining cookies.

7. Sprinkle powdered sugar over hollow cookies. Spread jam evenly onto the solid cookies; top with hollow cookies.

Use your favorite jams to vary the flavor and color of these beauties.

Orange-Pecan Biscotti

MAKES: 2 DOZEN HANDS-ON: 45 MIN. TOTAL: 2 HOURS 15 MIN.

4   large eggs
1   cup sugar
1 ½   Tbsp. loosely packed orange zest
2   Tbsp. vegetable oil
1   tsp. vanilla extract

1   tsp. almond extract
3 ⅓   cups all-purpose flour
2   tsp. baking powder
1   cup chopped pecans

1. Beat eggs and sugar at high speed with an electric mixer 5 minutes or until foamy. Add orange zest, oil, and extracts, beating until blended.
2. Combine flour and baking powder; add to sugar mixture, beating well. Fold in pecans. Cover and freeze 30 minutes or until firm.
3. Preheat oven to 325°. Lightly grease a baking sheet with cooking spray. Divide dough in half; shape each portion into an 8- x 5-inch log on baking sheet.
4. Bake at 325° for 25 minutes or until firm. Cool on baking sheet 5 minutes. Remove to wire racks to cool.
5. Cut each log diagonally into ½-inch slices with a serrated knife. Place on greased baking sheets.
6. Bake at 325° for 15 minutes. Turn cookies over, and bake 15 more minutes. Remove cookies to wire racks to cool.

Chocolate-Dipped Orange-Pecan Biscotti: Prepare Orange-Pecan Biscotti recipe as directed. Dip ends of biscotti in melted bittersweet chocolate and sprinkle with chopped pecans. Refrigerate until chocolate is set.

Use a long serrated knife to cut the biscotti in a sawing motion in order to get the prettiest slices.

Sugar Cookie Cutouts

We think ⅛ inch is the perfect thickness for a crisp, buttery cookie,
but this dough can be rolled to ¼-inch thick if you prefer a soft texture.

MAKES: **ABOUT 4 DOZEN** HANDS-ON: **30 MIN.** TOTAL: **2 HOURS 30 MIN.**

---

4 cups all-purpose flour	**Desired Holiday Glaze (recipes below):**
1 tsp. baking powder	**Eggnog Glaze**
½ tsp. kosher salt	**Chicory Coffee Glaze**
2 cups granulated sugar	**Key Lime Glaze**
1¼ cups butter, softened	**Mulled Wine Glaze**
2 tsp. vanilla extract	**Decorations:**
2 large eggs	**Sparkling sugars**
Parchment paper	**Silver BBs (Dragees)**

1. Stir together first 3 ingredients.
2. Beat sugar and next 2 ingredients at medium speed with an electric mixer 2 to 3 minutes or until creamy. Add eggs, 1 at a time, beating after each addition. Gradually add flour mixture, beating just until blended.
3. Divide dough into 4 equal portions; flatten each into a ½-inch-thick disk. Wrap each in plastic wrap; chill 30 minutes.
4. Working with 1 disk at a time, place on a lightly floured surface; roll to ¼-inch thickness. Cut with a 3-inch round cutter. Place 1 inch apart on 2 parchment paper-lined baking sheets. Chill 30 minutes.
5. Preheat oven to 350°. Bake 10 minutes or until edges begin to brown, switching baking sheets halfway through. Cool on baking sheets 10 minutes; transfer to wire racks, and cool completely. Glaze and decorate as desired.

Note: Total time does not include glazes.

4 Holiday Glazes

Each recipe makes about 1¼ cups, enough to glaze 4 dozen cookies.

Eggnog Glaze: Stir together 2 cups powdered sugar, 3 Tbsp. plus 2 tsp. whipping cream, 1 Tbsp. bourbon, ¼ tsp. kosher salt, and ¼ tsp. freshly grated nutmeg until smooth. Stir in up to 2 tsp. water, 1 tsp. at a time, until desired consistency.

Chicory Coffee Glaze: Stir together 2 cups powdered sugar, 2 Tbsp. strong brewed chicory coffee, 2 Tbsp. whipping cream, and ¼ tsp. kosher salt until smooth. Stir in up to 2 tsp. water, 1 tsp. at a time, until desired consistency. Garnish with crushed coffee beans.

Key Lime Glaze: Stir together 2 cups powdered sugar, 2 tsp. lime zest, 2 Tbsp. Key lime juice, 2 Tbsp. sweetened condensed milk, and ¼ tsp. kosher salt until smooth. Stir in up to 2 tsp. water, 1 tsp. at a time, until desired consistency.

Mulled Wine Glaze: Bring 1 cup red wine (such as Merlot), 1 Tbsp. light brown sugar, 1 (4- x ½-inch) orange peel strip, and ⅛ tsp. each ground allspice, ground cloves, ground nutmeg, and ground cinnamon to a boil in a saucepan over high heat; boil 7 to 10 minutes or until reduced to ¼ cup. Remove from heat, and stir in ¼ tsp. kosher salt until dissolved. Discard orange peel, and stir in 2 cups powdered sugar until smooth.

Peppermint Meringue Cookies

MAKES: ABOUT 7 ½ DOZEN   HANDS-ON: 30 MIN.   TOTAL: 5 HOURS 55 MIN.

6   large egg whites
1 ½ tsp. white vinegar
1 ½ cups sugar

1   tsp. peppermint extract
Red food coloring gel
Parchment paper

1. Preheat oven to 200°. Let egg whites stand 20 minutes. Beat egg whites at high speed with an electric mixer, using whisk attachment, until stiff peaks form. Reduce speed to medium. Add vinegar; add sugar, ½ cup at a time, and beat until blended. Beat 2 minutes. Beat in extract.

2. Paint 3 or 4 evenly spaced thin stripes of red food coloring gel on inside of a decorating bag, starting at tip and ending three-fourths of the way up bag. Gently spoon meringue into center of bag, filling three-fourths full. Snip end of bag. Pipe dollops of about 2 Tbsp. meringue onto 1 parchment paper-lined baking sheet, leaving 1 inch between each cookie. Repeat with remaining meringue, using a clean bag for each batch.

3. Bake at 200° for 2 hours. Turn off oven, and let meringues stand in oven until completely cool (about 3 hours).

Chocolate-Dipped Peppermint Meringues: Prepare recipe as directed. Melt 2 cups milk chocolate morsels in microwave according to package directions. Stir until smooth. Dip bottom of each cooled cookie in melted chocolate, and place on a parchment paper-lined baking sheet. Let stand 15 minutes or until chocolate sets.

Use food coloring gel in a squeeze bottle or a food-safe paintbrush to make lines in the piping bag. Once meringues have cooled, store them in an airtight container at room temperature.

Mississippi Mud Medallions

MAKES: **3 DOZEN** HANDS-ON: **25 MIN.** TOTAL: **40 MIN.**

6   whole graham crackers
Parchment paper
2   cups semisweet chocolate morsels

⅔   cup pecan halves, toasted
¼   cup chocolate-covered espresso beans

1. Place 3 whole graham crackers in a zip-top plastic freezer bag, and roll with a rolling pin until finely crushed. Spoon crushed graham crackers by level ½ teaspoonfuls 1 inch apart onto a parchment paper-lined baking sheet; flatten into 1-inch rounds. Break remaining crackers into ½-inch pieces.
2. Microwave chocolate morsels in a microwave-safe bowl at HIGH 30 seconds; stir. Microwave 10 to 20 more seconds or until melted and smooth, stirring at 10-second intervals.
3. Spoon melted chocolate into a large zip-top plastic freezer bag. Snip 1 corner of bag to make a small hole. Pipe chocolate over each graham cracker round.
4. Working quickly, press 1 (½-inch) graham cracker piece, 1 toasted pecan, and 1 espresso bean onto each chocolate round. Chill 15 minutes. Store in an airtight container at room temperature up to 1 week.

Note: To transfer chocolate into zip-top plastic freezer bag, nestle corner of bag in a 1-cup measuring cup and scrape melted chocolate into the opened bag, pooling it in the corner that is nestled in the measuring cup.

You can substitute mini marshmallows for espresso beans to make this cookie a little more kid-friendly.

Wreath Macaroons

Use your fingers to make a small hole in the center of each cookie.

MAKES: ABOUT 3 DOZEN HANDS-ON: 30 MIN. TOTAL: 1 HOUR 15 MIN.

14 oz. sweetened shredded coconut	Parchment paper
2 large egg whites	Holiday nonpareils
½ cup plus 2 tsp. sugar	Finely chopped candied cherries
1 tsp. vanilla extract	

1. Preheat oven to 350°. Combine first 4 ingredients. Drop by heaping tablespoonfuls onto 3 parchment paper-lined baking sheets, about 12 per sheet. Make a hole in center of each cookie; pinch each cookie into a wreath shape. Sprinkle with nonpareils and cherries.

2. Bake 2 baking sheets at 350° for 14 minutes. Rotate pans front to back, and bake 2 more minutes or until coconut begins to brown. Transfer parchment paper with cookies to wire racks; cool completely. Repeat with remaining baking sheet.

Apricot-Almond Thumbprints

MAKES: ABOUT 6 DOZEN HANDS-ON: 30 MIN. TOTAL: 1 HOUR 30 MIN.

2 cups butter, softened	4 ⅔ cups all-purpose flour
⅔ cup granulated sugar	1 ½ cups finely chopped sliced almonds
⅔ cup firmly packed light brown sugar	Parchment paper
1 tsp. almond extract	¾ cup apricot preserves
1 tsp. kosher salt	

1. Beat first 5 ingredients at medium speed with an electric mixer 3 to 5 minutes or until creamy. Add flour; beat just until blended.

2. Shape dough into 1-inch balls (about 1 Tbsp. per ball), and roll in almonds. Place 2 inches apart on 2 parchment paper lined-baking sheets. Press thumb or end of a wooden spoon into each ball, forming an indentation. Chill 20 minutes.

3. Preheat oven to 350°. Bake 15 minutes or until bottoms are light golden brown. Cool on baking sheets 10 minutes; transfer to wire racks, and cool 10 minutes. Spoon ½ tsp. apricot preserves into each indentation.

Wreath Macaroons

Peppermint Divinity Bars

MAKES: **32 BARS** HANDS-ON: **50 MIN.** TOTAL: **2 HOURS 10 MIN.**

3 cups all-purpose flour	Parchment paper
1 Tbsp. baking powder	¼ cup light corn syrup
1 tsp. kosher salt	2 large egg whites
1 vanilla bean	1 tsp. vanilla extract
1¼ cups butter, softened	¼ tsp. peppermint extract
2 cups sugar, divided	¾ cup crushed hard peppermint candies, divided

1. Preheat oven to 375°. Stir together first 3 ingredients.

2. Split vanilla bean; scrape seeds into bowl of a heavy-duty electric stand mixer. Add butter and 1 cup sugar; beat at medium speed 2 minutes or until creamy. Add flour mixture; beat until blended.

3. Line bottom and sides of a 13- x 9-inch pan with parchment paper, allowing 2 to 3 inches to extend over sides; lightly grease parchment paper. Press dough into bottom of prepared pan. Bake at 375° for 20 minutes or until edges are golden brown.

4. Meanwhile, stir together corn syrup, ¼ cup water, and remaining 1 cup sugar in a small saucepan over high heat, stirring just until sugar dissolves. Cook, without stirring, until a candy thermometer registers 250° (7 to 8 minutes).

5. While syrup cooks, beat egg whites at medium speed, using whisk attachment, until foamy.

6. When syrup reaches 250°, beat egg whites at medium-high speed until soft peaks form. While mixer is running, gradually add hot syrup to egg whites. Increase speed to high; beat until stiff peaks form. (Mixture should still be warm.) Add vanilla and peppermint extracts, and beat at medium speed just until combined. Fold in ½ cup peppermint candies.

7. Working quickly, spread mixture on warm cookie base, using a butter knife or offset spatula. Sprinkle with remaining ¼ cup crushed peppermints, and cool.

8. Lift mixture from pan, using parchment paper sides as handles; cut into 32 bars.

Make this recipe all the way through without stopping, spreading the warm divinity onto a still-warm cookie base. If the divinity is too cool, it will tear the cookie base as you spread it.

Espresso Shortbread Cookies

MAKES: **ABOUT 4 DOZEN** HANDS-ON: **45 MIN.** TOTAL: **3 HOURS 15 MIN.**

1   cup butter, softened
½   cup granulated sugar
1   tsp. sea salt
1   tsp. vanilla extract
2   cups all-purpose flour

½   cup chocolate-covered espresso beans, chopped
1   Tbsp. finely ground espresso beans
Wax paper
7   Tbsp. Demerara or turbinado sugar, divided

1. Beat first 3 ingredients at medium speed with a heavy-duty electric stand mixer 2 to 3 minutes or until light and fluffy. Stir in vanilla.

2. Stir together flour and next 2 ingredients in a medium bowl. Gradually add to butter mixture, beating just until blended; stop to scrape bowl as needed. (Do not overmix.)

3. Divide dough in half. Turn 1 dough portion out onto wax paper, and shape into a 10- x 2-inch log. Sprinkle log with 3 Tbsp. Demerara sugar, and roll log back and forth to adhere. Repeat with remaining dough portion and 3 Tbsp. Demerara sugar. Wrap logs in plastic wrap, and chill 2 to 3 hours.

4. Preheat oven to 350°. Cut chilled dough into ¼-inch-thick slices, and place 1 inch apart on 2 lightly greased baking sheets. Sprinkle 1 ½ tsp. Demerara sugar over cookies on each sheet.

5. Bake, in batches, at 350° for 12 to 15 minutes or until golden around edges, switching baking sheets halfway through.

6. Transfer to wire racks; cool 5 minutes. Serve immediately, or cool completely. Store in an airtight container at room temperature up to 4 days.

If you're a true coffee connoisseur or enjoy the savory taste of coffee with chocolate, you'll enjoy Espresso Shortbread Cookies.

Peppermint-Pretzel Bark

Peppermint-Pretzel Bark

Make even larger quantities for gifting this easy microwave treat by skipping the jelly-roll pan and covering your counter with parchment. It'll take longer to harden at room temperature, but you can make large batches without pans or the refrigerator.

MAKES: **12 SERVINGS** HANDS-ON: **15 MIN.** TOTAL: **20 MIN.**

1   (16-oz.) package vanilla candy coating, chopped
½   tsp. peppermint extract
Parchment paper

1   cup coarsely chopped pretzel sticks
⅔   cup coarsely chopped peppermint candy canes

1. Microwave candy coating in a 1-qt. microwave-safe glass bowl at MEDIUM (50% power) 1 minute; stir. Microwave until melted and smooth, stirring at 30-second intervals. Stir in peppermint extract.
2. Spread half of melted candy coating about ⅛ inch thick in a parchment paper-lined jelly-roll pan. Sprinkle ½ cup chopped pretzels and ⅓ cup chopped candy canes over melted candy coating, and press into coating. Repeat procedure with remaining ingredients on another parchment paper-lined jelly-roll pan. Chill 5 minutes or until cool and firm. Break into pieces.

Note: We tested with Log House Candiquik Vanilla Candy Coating and Nielsen-Massey Pure Peppermint Extract.

Milk Chocolate Peppermint Bark

Do not freeze. Frozen chocolate will get a powdery, chalky look called bloom.

MAKES: **2 ¾ LB.** HANDS-ON: **25 MIN.** TOTAL: **6 HOURS 25 MIN.**

Parchment paper
1   tsp. butter
3   (11.5-oz.) packages milk chocolate morsels
12   cream-and-mint filled chocolate sandwich
     cookies, broken into pieces

1   cup small pretzel sticks
1 ¼ cups coarsely chopped soft peppermint candies

1. Line a (15- x 10-inch) jelly-roll pan with parchment paper; grease with 1 tsp. butter.
2. Microwave chocolate in a large microwave-safe bowl at HIGH 1 to 2 minutes or until smooth, stirring at 45-second intervals.
3. Gently stir cookies, pretzels, and ¾ cup peppermint candies into chocolate mixture. Spread mixture in prepared pan. Sprinkle with remaining ½ cup peppermint candies.
4. Let stand until firm (about 6 hours). Break or cut bark into pieces. Store in an airtight container in a cool place up to 3 days.

Lemon Meltaways

MAKES: **ABOUT 3 ½ DOZEN** HANDS-ON: **30 MIN.** TOTAL: **2 HOURS**

¾ cup plus 2 Tbsp. butter, softened
1 ½ cups powdered sugar, divided
1 Tbsp. loosely packed lemon zest
2 Tbsp. fresh lemon juice

1 ½ cups all-purpose flour
¼ cup cornstarch
¼ tsp. table salt
Parchment paper

1. Beat butter at medium speed with a heavy-duty electric stand mixer until creamy. Add ½ cup powdered sugar; beat at medium speed until light and fluffy. Stir in zest and juice. Whisk together flour and next 2 ingredients. Gradually add flour mixture to butter mixture, beating at low speed just until blended. Cover and chill 1 hour.

2. Preheat oven to 350°. Drop dough by level spoonfuls 2 inches apart onto parchment paper-lined baking sheets, using a 1-inch cookie scoop.

3. Bake at 350° for 13 minutes or until lightly browned around edges. Cool on baking sheets 5 minutes.

4. Toss together warm cookies and remaining 1 cup powdered sugar in a small bowl.

You'll use just a tad less than two sticks of butter to make these delicate little gems.

Mocha-Espresso Cream Pie

Mocha-Espresso Cream Pie is a chocolate-lover's dream. A crunchy cookie crust is filled with a decadent chocolate filling before being topped off with Coffee Whipped Cream.

MAKES: 6 TO 8 SERVINGS HANDS-ON: 20 MIN.
TOTAL: 5 HOURS 5 MIN., INCLUDING COFFEE WHIPPED CREAM

CRUST
1	(9-oz.) package chocolate wafers
½	cup finely chopped toasted pecans
½	cup butter, melted

TOPPING
Coffee Whipped Cream (recipe below)

FILLING
⅔	cup sugar
¼	cup cornstarch
2	Tbsp. instant espresso
2	cups half-and-half
4	large egg yolks
2	oz. bittersweet chocolate baking squares, chopped
2	Tbsp. butter

Garnish: dark chocolate curls

1. Prepare Crust: Preheat oven to 350°. Pulse chocolate wafers in a food processor 8 to 10 times or until finely crushed. Stir together wafer crumbs, pecans, and butter. Press on bottom, up sides, and onto lip of a lightly greased 9-inch pie plate. Bake 10 minutes. Cool completely (about 30 minutes).
2. Prepare Filling: Whisk together sugar and next 2 ingredients in a large saucepan. Whisk together half-and-half and egg yolks in a large bowl. Gradually whisk egg mixture into sugar mixture; bring to a boil over medium heat, whisking constantly. Boil 1 minute, whisking constantly; remove from heat.
3. Microwave chocolate in a small bowl at HIGH 1 ½ minutes or until melted, stirring at 30-second intervals. Whisk 2 Tbsp. butter and melted chocolate into sugar mixture; spoon into prepared crust. Place plastic wrap directly onto filling (to prevent a film from forming). Chill 4 to 24 hours. Top with Coffee Whipped Cream just before serving. Garnish, if desired.

Coffee Whipped Cream

Coffee liqueur spikes the Coffee Whipped Cream that tops our Mocha-Espresso Cream Pie.

2	cups heavy cream	⅓	cup sugar
1	Tbsp. coffee liqueur		

Beat heavy cream and coffee liqueur at medium-high speed with an electric mixer until foamy; gradually add sugar, beating until soft peaks form. Makes about 3 ½ cups.

Note: We tested with Kahlúa coffee liqueur.

Sliced Sweet Potato Pie

We love the layered look of this ever-so-sweet streusel-topped treat.
Serve alongside ice cream for a decadent treat.

MAKES: 8 SERVINGS HANDS-ON: 20 MIN.
TOTAL: 3 HOURS 15 MIN., INCLUDING STREUSEL TOPPING

½ (14.1-oz.) package refrigerated piecrusts
2½ lb. small, slender sweet potatoes, peeled and cut into ⅛-inch to ¼-inch rounds
½ cup granulated sugar
2 (4- x 1-inch) orange peel strips
½ cup firmly packed light brown sugar
2 Tbsp. all-purpose flour
2 tsp. pumpkin pie spice
1 tsp. loosely packed orange zest
½ tsp. table salt
Streusel Topping (recipe below)

1. Preheat oven to 375°. Fit piecrust into a 9-inch deep-dish pie plate; fold edges under, and crimp. Bring potatoes, next 2 ingredients, and 1 cup water to a boil in a Dutch oven. Cover, reduce heat to medium, and simmer 6 minutes or until potatoes are just tender.
2. Transfer potatoes to a large colander, reserving cooking liquid. Rinse potatoes with cold water. Transfer cooking liquid and orange peel strips to a small saucepan, and bring to a boil over medium-high heat. Reduce heat to medium, and simmer, stirring occasionally, 10 to 12 minutes or until reduced to ¼ cup. Reserve 2 Tbsp. potato-orange liquid; discard remaining liquid.
3. Transfer potatoes to a bowl; toss with brown sugar, next 4 ingredients, and reserved 2 Tbsp. potato-orange liquid. Spoon into crust; sprinkle with Streusel Topping.
4. Bake at 375° for 1 hour and 5 minutes to 1 hour and 15 minutes, shielding with aluminum foil after 30 minutes to prevent excessive browning. Cool completely.

Streusel Topping

Streusel Topping takes an ordinary pie to extraordinary.

¾ cup coarsely chopped pecans
¼ cup plus 1 Tbsp. all-purpose flour
¼ cup firmly packed light brown sugar
3 Tbsp. butter, melted
1 Tbsp. granulated sugar
¼ tsp. pumpkin pie spice
⅛ tsp. table salt

Stir together pecans, flour, brown sugar, melted butter, granulated sugar, pumpkin pie spice, and table salt. Let stand 30 minutes. Crumble into small pieces. Makes 1¼ cups.

Coconut-Pumpkin Chiffon Pie

MAKES: 8 TO 10 SERVINGS   HANDS-ON: 35 MIN.   TOTAL: 2 HOURS 35 MIN.

½ cup milk

2 envelopes unflavored gelatin

1 (15-oz.) can pumpkin

1 tsp. ground cinnamon

½ tsp. table salt

½ tsp. ground nutmeg

½ tsp. ground ginger

4 large pasteurized eggs, separated

1 cup plus 3 Tbsp. sugar, divided

1¼ cups sweetened shredded coconut, divided

1 cup graham cracker crumbs

5 Tbsp. butter, melted

2 cups heavy cream

2 tsp. vanilla extract

1. Preheat oven to 350°. Whisk together milk and gelatin in a 3-qt. saucepan; let stand 1 minute. Cook over medium heat, stirring constantly, 1 minute or until the gelatin dissolves. Stir in pumpkin, next 4 ingredients, egg yolks, and ½ cup sugar. Cook, stirring constantly, 5 to 7 minutes or until slightly thickened. (Do not boil.) Transfer to a bowl; chill 40 minutes or to room temperature, stirring halfway through.

2. Meanwhile, place coconut in a single layer on a baking sheet, and bake at 350° for 8 to 10 minutes or until golden, stirring occasionally.

3. Stir together graham cracker crumbs, butter, 1 Tbsp. sugar, and 1 cup coconut. Press mixture into a 10-inch pie plate. Freeze 10 minutes or until ready to use.

4. Beat egg whites at high speed with a heavy-duty electric stand mixer, using whisk attachment, 8 minutes or until soft peaks form. Add ¼ cup sugar, and beat 2 to 3 minutes or until stiff peaks form.

5. Gradually fold egg whites into pumpkin mixture. Pour into crust. Chill 2 hours or until set.

6. Beat cream and vanilla at medium speed 1 to 2 minutes or until soft peaks form. Add remaining 6 Tbsp. sugar, and beat 1 to 2 minutes or until stiff peaks form. Top pie with cream mixture and remaining ¼ cup coconut. Serve immediately.

Make and refrigerate without the topping a day ahead. Whip and add the topping before serving.

Butterscotch Meringue Pie with Pecan Crust

We won't revoke your pie credentials if you use a purchased piecrust in this recipe, but we love the way the homemade crust's nutty flavor elevates the caramel filling so much that we recommend you give it a try. A few rules of the road: Be sure to finely grind the pecans to ensure the crust holds together. And if the crust tears just a bit, don't be alarmed. As with all piecrusts, you can easily press it back together with your fingertips or use extra scraps for patchwork.

MAKES: 8 SERVINGS HANDS-ON: 55 MIN. TOTAL: 8 HOURS 5 MIN.

CRUST
½   cup chopped pecans
1 ¼   cups all-purpose flour
2   Tbsp. granulated sugar
½   cup cold butter, cut into ½-inch pieces
2   Tbsp. ice-cold water
1   tsp. vanilla extract
Wax paper
Parchment paper

FILLING
2   cups firmly packed light brown sugar
⅔   cup all-purpose flour
½   tsp. table salt
2 ½   cups milk
6   egg yolks, lightly beaten
½   cup butter, cut into 1-inch pieces
2   tsp. vanilla extract

MERINGUE
6   large egg whites
1   tsp. vanilla extract
¼   tsp. cream of tartar
6   Tbsp. granulated sugar

1. Prepare Crust: Pulse pecans in a food processor 10 to 12 times or until finely chopped. Transfer pecans to a small bowl. Pulse 1 ¼ cups flour and 2 Tbsp. granulated sugar in processor 2 or 3 times to combine. Add ½-inch butter pieces, and pulse 10 to 12 times or until mixture resembles coarse meal. Add pecans, and pulse 2 or 3 times to combine. With processor running, pour 2 Tbsp. ice-cold water and 1 tsp. vanilla through food chute, and process just until dough comes together. Transfer dough to a lightly floured surface, and shape into a disk. Wrap disk in plastic wrap, and chill 30 minutes.

2. Preheat oven to 350°. Place dough disk between 2 sheets of lightly floured wax paper, and roll to a 12-inch circle. Fit piecrust into a 9-inch deep-dish pie plate; fold edges under, and crimp. Prick bottom and sides of dough with a fork; line dough with parchment paper, and fill with pie weights or dried beans.

3. Bake at 350° for 20 minutes. Remove weights and parchment paper, and bake 10 to 12 more minutes or until browned. Cool completely on a wire rack (about 1 hour).

4. Prepare Filling: Whisk together brown sugar and next 2 ingredients in a medium saucepan. Gradually whisk in milk. Cook over medium heat, whisking constantly, 8 to 9 minutes or until mixture is smooth and begins to thicken.

5. Gradually whisk about one-fourth of hot sugar mixture into egg yolks; gradually whisk egg yolk mixture into hot sugar mixture, and cook, whisking constantly, 2 to 3 more minutes or until mixture is thick and smooth and just begins to bubble. Remove from heat, and whisk in 1-inch butter pieces and 2 tsp. vanilla. Pour filling into prepared pie crust.

6. Prepare Meringue: Beat egg whites and next 2 ingredients at high speed with an electric mixer until foamy. Gradually add 6 Tbsp. granulated sugar, 1 Tbsp. at a time, beating until stiff peaks form and sugar dissolves. Spread meringue over hot filling, sealing edges.

7. Bake at 350° for 10 to 12 minutes or until golden brown. Remove from oven to a wire rack, and cool completely (about 2 hours). Chill 4 to 6 hours before serving.

Pumpkin Cheesecake Tart with Honey Swiss Meringue

Begin with a toasted pecan crust, layer with cream cheese and a classic pumpkin filling, and then top with a creamy meringue.

MAKES: 6 TO 8 SERVINGS HANDS-ON: 45 MIN. TOTAL: 13 HOURS 10 MIN., INCLUDING MERINGUE

TART CRUST
- ½ cup chopped toasted pecans
- 7 Tbsp. butter, softened
- 1 cup powdered sugar
- ¼ tsp. table salt
- 1 large egg
- ¼ tsp. vanilla extract
- 2 cups all-purpose flour

CREAM CHEESE LAYER
- 2 (8-oz.) packages cream cheese, softened
- ½ cup granulated sugar
- 1 large egg
- 1 tsp. loosely packed orange zest

PUMPKIN LAYER
- 1 (15-oz.) can pumpkin
- 3 large eggs
- ½ cup heavy cream
- ⅓ cup firmly packed light brown sugar
- 1½ tsp. pumpkin pie spice
- ½ tsp. table salt

TOPPING
Honey Swiss Meringue (recipe below)

1. Prepare Tart Crust: Process pecans in a food processor 10 to 12 seconds or until finely ground.
2. Beat butter at medium speed with an electric mixer 1 minute or until creamy. Gradually add powdered sugar and salt. Add egg, beating just until blended; stir in vanilla. Stir together flour and processed pecans; add to butter mixture, beating at low speed until mixture is no longer crumbly and forms a ball, pulling away from sides of bowl. Press dough on bottom and up sides of a 9-inch deep-dish tart pan with a removable bottom. Chill until firm.
3. Preheat oven to 350°. Line crust with aluminum foil, and fill with pie weights. Bake 20 minutes. Remove weights and foil; bake 12 to 14 more minutes or until crust is light brown. Cool completely on a wire rack (about 30 minutes). Increase oven temperature to 425°.
4. Prepare Cream Cheese Layer: Beat cream cheese, sugar, and egg at low speed until smooth. Stir in orange zest. Spread over bottom of crust.
5. Prepare Pumpkin Layer: Whisk together pumpkin and next 5 ingredients until smooth; pour over cream cheese layer in crust. Cover tart edges with foil. Bake at 425° for 15 minutes; reduce temperature to 350°, and bake 45 to 55 more minutes or until a knife inserted in center of pumpkin layer comes out clean. Transfer to a wire rack, and cool completely (about 1 hour). Cover and chill 8 to 12 hours.
6. Prepare Topping: Gently blot any moisture that collected on top of tart during chilling with a paper towel. Spread Honey Swiss Meringue over tart. Brown meringue using a kitchen torch, holding torch 1 to 2 inches from meringue and moving torch back and forth.

Honey Swiss Meringue

- ⅔ cup clover honey
- 4 large egg whites
- ¼ tsp. table salt

Whisk together honey, egg whites, and salt. Pour water to a depth of 1 inch into bottom of a double boiler over medium heat; bring to a boil. Reduce heat, and simmer; place honey mixture in top of double boiler over simmering water. Cook, whisking constantly, 10 to 12 minutes or until mixture reaches 160°. Quickly transfer mixture to bowl of a heavy-duty electric stand mixer, and beat, using whisk attachment, until stiff peaks form. Makes about 4 cups.

Cinderella Cheesecake

This recipe is from Savor the Moment *by the Junior League of Boca Raton.*

MAKES: 10 TO 12 SERVINGS HANDS-ON: 45 MIN.
TOTAL: 11 HOURS 5 MIN., INCLUDING SOUR CREAM TOPPING

BROWNIE CRUST

3	(1-oz.) unsweetened chocolate baking squares
¼	cup unsalted butter
½	cup sifted all-purpose flour
⅛	tsp. table salt
⅛	tsp. baking powder
2	large eggs
1	cup firmly packed light brown sugar
1½	tsp. vanilla extract
½	(1-oz.) bittersweet chocolate baking square, finely chopped

CHEESECAKE FILLING AND TOPPING

1½	(8-oz.) packages cream cheese, softened
1	cup firmly packed light brown sugar
3	large eggs
½	cup sour cream
1⅓	cups creamy peanut butter
	Sour Cream Topping (recipe below)
	Chocolate curls

1. Prepare Brownie Crust: Preheat oven to 350°. Microwave first 2 ingredients in a small microwave-safe bowl at MEDIUM (50% power) 1½ minutes or until melted, stirring at 30-second intervals. Stir together flour, salt, and baking powder in a bowl.

2. Beat 2 eggs and 1 cup brown sugar at medium-high speed with an electric mixer 3 to 4 minutes or until batter forms thin ribbons when beaters are lifted. Add vanilla, bittersweet chocolate, and melted chocolate mixture, and beat just until blended. Stir in flour mixture just until combined.

3. Spread 1 cup brownie mixture on bottom of a greased and floured 9-inch springform pan. Bake at 350° on center oven rack 13 to 15 minutes or until set. Cool on a wire rack 10 minutes; freeze 15 minutes. Remove from freezer; spread remaining brownie batter up sides of pan to ¼ inch from top, sealing batter to bottom crust.

4. Prepare Filling: Beat cream cheese and 1 cup brown sugar at medium speed with a heavy-duty electric stand mixer until blended. Add 3 eggs, 1 at a time, beating just until yellow disappears after each addition. Beat in sour cream just until blended. Beat in peanut butter until blended.

5. Pour filling into prepared crust. (Mixture will not completely fill crust.) Bake at 350° for 35 minutes or until center is almost set.

6. Remove from oven. Spread Sour Cream Topping over center of cheesecake, leaving a 2-inch border around edge. Bake at 350° for 1 more minute. Remove from oven; gently run a knife around edge of cheesecake to loosen. Cool completely on a wire rack.

7. Cover and chill 8 to 12 hours. Remove sides of pan. Top with chocolate curls.

Note: We tested with Jif peanut butter.

Sour Cream Topping

¾	cup sour cream	2	tsp. sugar

Stir together sour cream and sugar in a small bowl until smooth. Makes ¾ cup.

Buttermilk-Glazed Mini Fig Cakes

Muffin pans make the perfect baking vessels for these little fig cakes.

MAKES: 20 MINI CAKES HANDS-ON: 15 MIN.
TOTAL: 1 HOUR 30 MIN., INCLUDING GLAZE AND SAUCE

2	cups all-purpose flour	1	cup buttermilk
1	cup sugar	1	tsp. vanilla extract
1	tsp. baking soda	1	cup fig preserves
1	tsp. table salt	½	cup chopped toasted pecans
1	tsp. ground cinnamon		Buttermilk Glaze (recipe below)
1	tsp. ground cloves		Vanilla Hard Sauce (recipe below)
1	cup vegetable oil		Garnishes: fresh rosemary sprigs,
3	large eggs		quartered fresh figs

1. Preheat oven to 350°. Stir together flour and next 5 ingredients in a large bowl. Gradually add oil, beating at medium speed with an electric mixer until blended. Add eggs, 1 at a time, beating until blended. Add buttermilk and vanilla, beating until blended. Fold in preserves and pecans.
2. Spoon batter into 2 lightly greased (12-cup) muffin pans, filling 20 muffin cups about three-fourths full.
3. Bake at 350° for 15 to 18 minutes or until a wooden pick inserted in center comes out clean. Cool in pans 5 minutes. Invert cakes onto wire racks. Cool 15 minutes.
4. Drizzle cakes with Buttermilk Glaze. Cool 10 minutes. Pipe Vanilla Hard Sauce onto warm cakes. Garnish, if desired, and serve.

Buttermilk Glaze

Our Mini Fig Cakes glisten with the warmed Buttermilk Glaze that's drizzled over the top of each one.

½	cup sugar	2	tsp. cornstarch
¼	cup buttermilk	¼	tsp. baking soda
¼	cup butter	1½	tsp. vanilla extract

1. Bring sugar and next 4 ingredients to a boil in a small saucepan over medium heat, stirring often.
2. Immediately remove mixture from heat, and cool 10 minutes. Stir in vanilla. Makes about ¾ cup.

Vanilla Hard Sauce

1	vanilla bean*	1	cup butter, softened
2	cups sifted powdered sugar		

1. Split vanilla bean lengthwise, and scrape seeds into a large bowl. Stir in powdered sugar.
2. Beat butter into sugar mixture at medium speed with an electric mixer until blended. Makes about 1½ cups.

*1 Tbsp. vanilla extract may be substituted. Omit Step 1. Stir extract into mixture after beating butter and sugar together in Step 2.

Red Velvet Marble Bundt Cake

*The trick to creating looping swirls is to gently layer the batter around the Bundt pan
with a small cookie scoop. No need to swirl with a knife; it will marble as it bakes.*

MAKES: 10 TO 12 SERVINGS   HANDS-ON: 30 MIN.   TOTAL: 2 HOURS 45 MIN., INCLUDING GLAZE

1 cup butter, softened	¾ cup milk
½ cup shortening	1 tsp. vanilla extract
2 ½ cups sugar	1 Tbsp. unsweetened cocoa
6 large eggs	1 Tbsp. red liquid food coloring
3 cups all-purpose flour	Snowy White Vanilla Glaze (recipe below)
1 tsp. baking powder	Garnishes: mint sprigs, red-and-white fondant balls
½ tsp. table salt	

1. Preheat oven to 325°. Beat butter and shortening at medium speed with a heavy-duty electric stand mixer until creamy. Gradually add sugar, beating until light and fluffy. Add eggs, 1 at a time, beating just until blended after each addition.

2. Stir together flour and next 2 ingredients. Add to butter mixture alternately with milk, beginning and ending with flour mixture. Beat at low speed until blended after each addition. Stir in vanilla. Transfer 2½ cups batter to a 2-qt. bowl; stir in cocoa and food coloring.

3. Drop 2 scoops of plain batter into a greased and floured 10-inch (16-cup) Bundt pan, using a small cookie scoop (about 1 ½ inches); top with 1 scoop of red velvet batter. Repeat around entire pan, covering bottom completely. Continue layering batters in pan as directed until all batter is used.

4. Bake at 325° for 1 hour to 1 hour and 5 minutes or until a wooden pick inserted in center comes out clean. Cool in pan on a wire rack 10 minutes; remove from pan to wire rack, and cool completely (about 1 hour). Drizzle with Snowy White Vanilla Glaze. Garnish, if desired.

Snowy White Vanilla Glaze

A simple Snowy White Vanilla Glaze graces the top of our Red Velvet Marble Bundt Cake.

2 ½ cups powdered sugar	1 tsp. vanilla extract
3 Tbsp. plus 1 tsp. milk	

Whisk together powdered sugar, milk, and vanilla until smooth. Makes about 1 cup.

Peppermint Ice-Cream Cake

This is a towering peppermint-lover's dream.
Clear about 14 square inches of room in your freezer before you begin.

MAKES: 10 TO 12 SERVINGS HANDS-ON: 45 MIN.
TOTAL: 1 HOUR 40 MIN., PLUS 1 DAY FOR FREEZING

CHIFFON CAKE LAYERS
4   (8-in.) round disposable aluminum foil cake pans
Wax paper
2   cups sifted cake flour
½   tsp. table salt
1¼   cups granulated sugar, divided
½   cup canola oil
½   cup milk
1   tsp. vanilla extract
4   large egg yolks
8   large egg whites
1   tsp. cream of tartar

PEPPERMINT ICE-CREAM LAYERS
3   (8-in.) round disposable aluminum foil cake pans
½   gal. vanilla ice cream, softened
1   cup finely crushed hard peppermint candies (about 40 pieces)

WHIPPED CREAM FROSTING
3   cups heavy cream
1   tsp. vanilla extract
½   cup powdered sugar

GARNISH
Crushed hard peppermint candies

1. Prepare Chiffon Cake Layers: Preheat oven to 325°. Lightly grease bottoms of 4 disposable cake pans; line bottoms with wax paper, and lightly grease.
2. Whisk together flour, salt, and 1 cup sugar in bowl of a heavy-duty electric stand mixer.
3. Whisk together oil and next 3 ingredients; add to flour mixture, and beat at medium speed 1 to 2 minutes or until smooth.
4. Beat egg whites at medium speed until foamy. Add cream of tartar; beat at high speed until soft peaks form. Gradually add remaining ¼ cup sugar, 1 Tbsp. at a time, beating until stiff peaks form and sugar dissolves. Gently stir one-fourth egg white mixture into flour mixture; gently fold in remaining egg white mixture. Divide batter among prepared pans, spreading with an offset spatula. Sharply tap pans once on counter to remove air bubbles.
5. Bake at 325° for 14 to 16 minutes or until a wooden pick inserted in center comes out clean. Cool in pans on wire racks 10 minutes. Remove from pans to wire racks; discard wax paper. Cool completely. Wrap layers in plastic wrap, and freeze 12 hours.
6. Meanwhile, prepare Ice-Cream Layers: Line 3 disposable cake pans with plastic wrap, allowing 6 to 8 inches to extend over sides. Stir together ice cream and candies in a large bowl. Divide mixture among prepared pans (about 2½ cups per pan), spreading to within ½ inch of sides of pans. (The cake layers shrink a little as they cool, so this helps ensure that the ice-cream layers will be the same size.) Cover with plastic wrap, and freeze 12 to 24 hours.
7. Assemble Cake: Remove plastic wrap. Place 1 layer of cake on a serving plate; top with 1 layer of ice cream. Repeat with remaining layers of cake and ice cream, ending with cake on top. Wrap entire cake with plastic wrap, and freeze 12 to 24 hours.
8. Prepare Frosting: Beat cream and vanilla at medium speed until foamy. Increase speed to medium-high, and gradually add powdered sugar, beating until stiff peaks form. (Do not overbeat or cream will be grainy.) Remove cake from freezer. Spread top and sides with Whipped Cream Frosting. Serve immediately, or freeze up to 12 hours. Garnish, if desired. Store in freezer.

Carrot Cake with Chèvre Frosting

MAKES: **8 SERVINGS** HANDS-ON: **40 MIN.** TOTAL: **2 HOURS 35 MIN.**

CAKE
Parchment paper
2   cups all-purpose flour
2   tsp. baking soda
1   tsp. table salt
1   tsp. ground cinnamon
2   cups sugar
1 ¼   cups canola oil
3   large eggs
3   cups grated carrots
1   (8-oz.) can crushed pineapple in juice, drained
1 ¼   cups coarsely chopped walnuts, toasted
2   Tbsp. minced fresh ginger

FROSTING
8   oz. goat cheese or cream cheese, softened
½   cup butter, softened
1   (16-oz.) package powdered sugar
1   vanilla bean

GARNISHES
Walnuts, carrot curls

1. Prepare Cake: Preheat oven to 350°. Grease 2 (8-inch) round cake pans; line bottoms with parchment paper, and grease and flour paper.
2. Stir together flour and next 3 ingredients.
3. Whisk together sugar and oil in a large bowl until well blended. Add eggs, 1 at a time, whisking until blended after each addition. Add flour mixture, stirring just until blended. Fold in carrots and next 3 ingredients. Spoon batter into prepared cake pans.
4. Bake at 350° for 40 to 45 minutes or until a wooden pick inserted in center comes out clean. Cool in pans on wire racks 15 minutes. Remove from pans to wire racks; discard parchment paper. Cool completely (about 1 hour).
5. Prepare Frosting: Beat goat cheese and butter at medium speed with an electric mixer 2 to 3 minutes or until creamy. Add powdered sugar, 1 cup at a time, beating at low speed until blended after each addition.
6. Split vanilla bean; scrape seeds into goat cheese mixture. Beat 30 seconds to 1 minute or until frosting is light and fluffy. Spread ½ cup frosting between cake layers; spread remaining frosting on top and sides of cake. Garnish, if desired.

Substituting goat cheese for the standard cream cheese gives this frosting an extra-tangy kick.

Ambrosia Coconut Cake

MAKES: 12 SERVINGS HANDS-ON: 30 MIN.
TOTAL: 11 HOURS, INCLUDING FILLING AND BUTTERCREAM

MAKE AHEAD TIP

Make the filling and frosting up to 2 days ahead. Then, build the cake, and chill up to 24 hours.

1	cup butter, softened		1	tsp. vanilla extract
2	cups sugar		¼	tsp. coconut extract
4	large eggs, separated		⅛	tsp. table salt
3	cups all-purpose flour			Vanilla Buttercream (recipe below)
1	Tbsp. baking powder			Ambrosia Filling (recipe below)
½	cup milk			Garnishes: sweetened flaked coconut, fresh
½	cup coconut milk			mint, maraschino cherries, orange slices

1. Preheat oven to 350°. Beat butter at medium speed with a heavy-duty electric stand mixer until fluffy; gradually add sugar, beating well. Add egg yolks, 1 at a time, beating just until blended after each addition.

2. Combine flour and baking powder; stir together milk and coconut milk. Add flour mixture to butter mixture alternately with milk mixture, beginning and ending with flour. Beat at low speed until blended after each addition. Stir in extracts.

3. Beat egg whites and salt at high speed until stiff peaks form. Stir about one-third egg whites into batter; fold in remaining egg whites. Spoon batter into 3 greased and floured 9-inch round cake pans.

4. Bake at 350° for 18 to 22 minutes or until a wooden pick inserted in center comes out clean. Cool in pans on wire racks 10 minutes; remove from pans to wire racks, and cool completely.

5. Place 1 cake layer on a serving platter. Spoon ⅓ cup Vanilla Buttercream into a zip-top plastic bag. Snip 1 corner of bag to make a small hole. Pipe a ring of frosting around cake layer just inside the top edge. Top with half of Ambrosia Filling, and spread to edge of ring. Top with a second cake layer. Repeat procedure with frosting and filling. Top with remaining cake layer, and spread frosting on top and sides of cake. Garnish, if desired.

Vanilla Buttercream

1	cup butter, softened		1	(32-oz.) package powdered sugar
1	tsp. vanilla extract		¾	to 1 cup heavy cream

Beat butter at medium speed with an electric mixer until creamy. Gradually add vanilla and 1 cup powdered sugar. Gradually add remaining powdered sugar alternately with cream, beating at low speed until blended after each addition. Beat at high speed until smooth. Makes 4 ½ cups.

Ambrosia Filling

1	navel orange		¾	cup heavy cream
1	(8-oz). can crushed pineapple in juice		3	large egg yolks
¾	cup sugar		2	Tbsp. butter
1	Tbsp. cornstarch		¼	tsp. coconut extract
¼	tsp. table salt		1	cup toasted sweetened flaked coconut

Grate zest from orange to equal 2 tsp. Peel and section orange; chop segments. Place orange and pineapple in a strainer, and drain. Whisk together sugar, cornstarch, and salt in a 3-qt. saucepan. Whisk in cream and egg yolks. Bring to a boil over medium heat, whisking constantly; boil 1 minute or until thickened. Remove from heat; whisk in butter and coconut extract. Stir in orange-pineapple mixture, coconut, and orange zest. Transfer to a bowl, place plastic wrap directly on filling, and chill 8 to 48 hours. Makes about 2 ¼ cups.

Red Velvet-White Chocolate Cheesecake

*This gorgeous cake marries two favorite holiday cake flavors: red velvet
and cheesecake, and gets topped with white chocolate frosting and candy "leaves."*

MAKES: 10 TO 12 SERVINGS HANDS-ON: 45 MIN. TOTAL: 13 HOURS 45 MIN.

CHEESECAKE LAYERS
- 2 (8-in.) round disposable aluminum foil cake pans
- 1 (12-oz.) package white chocolate morsels
- 5 (8-oz.) packages cream cheese, softened
- 1 cup granulated sugar
- 2 large eggs
- 1 Tbsp. vanilla extract

RED VELVET LAYERS
- 1 cup butter, softened
- 2 ½ cups granulated sugar
- 6 large eggs
- 3 cups all-purpose flour
- 3 Tbsp. unsweetened cocoa
- ¼ tsp. baking soda

- 1 (8-oz.) container sour cream
- 2 tsp. vanilla extract
- 2 (1-oz.) bottles red liquid food coloring
- 3 (8-in.) round disposable aluminum foil cake pans

WHITE CHOCOLATE FROSTING
- 2 (4-oz.) white chocolate baking bars, chopped
- ½ cup boiling water
- 1 cup butter, softened
- 1 (32-oz.) package powdered sugar, sifted
- ⅛ tsp. table salt

GARNISHES
Store-bought coconut candies, White Candy Leaves (page 267)

1. Prepare Cheesecake Layers: Preheat oven to 300°. Line bottom and sides of 2 disposable cake pans with aluminum foil, allowing 2 to 3 inches to extend over sides; lightly grease foil.

2. Microwave white chocolate morsels in a microwave-safe bowl according to package directions; cool 10 minutes.

3. Beat cream cheese and melted chocolate at medium speed with an electric mixer until creamy; gradually add 1 cup sugar, beating well. Add 2 eggs, 1 at a time, beating just until yellow disappears after each addition. Stir in 1 Tbsp. vanilla. Pour into prepared pans.

4. Bake at 300° for 30 to 35 minutes or until almost set. Turn oven off. Let cheesecakes stand in oven, with door closed, 30 minutes. Remove from oven to wire racks; cool completely (about 1 ½ hours). Cover and chill 8 hours, or freeze 24 hours to 2 days.

5. Prepare Red Velvet Layers: Preheat oven to 350°. Beat 1 cup butter at medium speed with a heavy-duty electric stand mixer until creamy. Gradually add 2 ½ cups sugar, beating until light and fluffy. Add 6 eggs, 1 at a time, beating just until blended after each addition.

6. Stir together flour and next 2 ingredients; add to butter mixture alternately with sour cream, beginning and ending with flour mixture. Beat at low speed just until blended after each addition. Stir in 2 tsp. vanilla; stir in food coloring. Spoon batter into 3 greased and floured 8-inch disposable cake pans.

7. Bake at 350° for 20 to 24 minutes or until a wooden pick inserted in center comes out clean. Cool in pans on wire racks 10 minutes. Remove from pans to wire racks; cool completely (about 1 hour).

8. Prepare Frosting: Whisk together chocolate and ½ cup boiling water until chocolate melts. Cool 20 minutes; chill 30 minutes.

9. Beat 1 cup butter and chilled chocolate mixture at low speed until blended. Beat at medium speed 1 minute. Increase speed to high; beat 2 to 3 minutes or until fluffy. Gradually add powdered sugar and salt, beating at low speed until blended. Increase speed to high; beat 1 to 2 minutes or until smooth and fluffy.

10. Assemble Cake: Place 1 layer Red Velvet on a serving platter. Top with 1 layer Cheesecake. Repeat with remaining layers of Red Velvet and Cheesecake, alternating and ending with Red Velvet on top. Spread top and sides of cake with White Chocolate Frosting. Store in refrigerator. Garnish, if desired.

Note: We tested with Confetteria Raffaello Almond Coconut Treats.

Cherries
Jubilee Cakes

White Candy Leaves

Accent the top of the Red Velvet-White Chocolate Cheesecake (page 264)
or other favorite holiday cake with White Candy Leaves.

MAKES: 12 LEAVES HANDS-ON: 15 MIN. TOTAL: 15 MIN.

Nontoxic leaves, such as bay leaves
About 2 oz. vanilla candy coating

Parchment paper

1. Select nontoxic leaves, such as bay leaves. Thoroughly wash the leaves, and pat dry. Melt vanilla candy coating in a saucepan over low heat until melted (about 3 minutes). Stir until smooth. Cool slightly. Working on parchment paper, spoon a ⅛-inch-thick layer of candy coating over backs of leaves, spreading to edges.
2. Transfer leaves gently, by their stems, to a clean sheet of parchment paper, resting them candy coating sides up; let stand until candy coating is firm (about 10 minutes). Gently grasp each leaf at stem end, and carefully peel the leaf away from the candy coating. Store candy leaves in a cold, dry place, such as an airtight container in the freezer, up to 1 week.
3. Handle leaves gently when garnishing, or they'll break or melt. Arrange candy leaves around the base of the cake and store-bought coconut candies in the center of the cake. Accent the top of the cake with additional candy leaves. For candy pearls, simply roll any remaining candy coating into balls, and let stand until dry.

Cherries Jubilee Cakes

Santa's secret: No one will ever guess these elegant little cakes
came from a box of white cake mix and a couple of cans of cherries.

MAKES: 10 CAKES HANDS-ON: 45 MIN. TOTAL: 2 HOURS

2   (14.5-oz.) cans pitted tart cherries in water
1   (15.25-oz.) package white cake mix
¾   cup sugar
3   Tbsp. cornstarch

1   (12-oz.) container frozen whipped topping, thawed
2   Tbsp. clear cherry brandy (optional)
Garnishes: powdered sugar, edible glitter stars

1. Preheat oven to 350°. Drain cherries, reserving ¾ cup liquid from cans. Coarsely chop ½ cup cherries, and drain well, pressing between paper towels to squeeze out excess juice.
2. Prepare cake mix batter according to package directions; stir chopped cherries into batter.
3. Lightly grease 2 (6-cup) jumbo muffin pans with cooking spray. Spoon batter into 10 muffin cups, filling two-thirds full.
4. Bake at 350° for 17 to 19 minutes or until a wooden pick inserted in center comes out clean. Cool completely in pans.
5. Meanwhile, bring remaining cherries, sugar, and reserved cherry liquid to a boil in a saucepan over medium-high heat. Reduce heat to low, and simmer, stirring constantly, 1 minute. Stir together cornstarch and 2 Tbsp. water until combined. Quickly stir cornstarch mixture into cherry mixture, and cook, stirring often, 2 minutes or until mixture begins to thicken. Remove from heat, and cool 15 minutes.
6. Hollow out a 2 ½-inch hole from the top of each muffin. Top each with about 2 Tbsp. cherry mixture.
7. Spoon whipped topping into a medium bowl. Stir in brandy, if desired, just before serving. Dollop mixture over cakes. Serve immediately, or chill 24 hours. Garnish, if desired.

Note: We tested with Oregon Fruit Products Pitted Red Tart Cherries in Water.

Cranberry Dreamsicle Trifle

MAKES: 10 TO 12 SERVINGS   HANDS-ON: 30 MIN.   TOTAL: 1 HOUR 15 MIN.

MAKE AHEAD TIP

This cake tastes better the longer it sits. Make this beauty up to one day before company arrives.

3 ½   cups frozen or fresh cranberries
¾   cup sugar
½   cup orange juice
2 ½   cups milk
⅔   cup sugar
1   Tbsp. orange zest
1   tsp. vanilla extract
3   large egg yolks
⅓   cup cornstarch
3   Tbsp. orange juice
1   (16-oz.) frozen pound cake, thawed
1 ½   cups whipping cream, whipped to soft peaks
Garnishes: fresh rosemary sprigs, white chocolate curls

1. Bring first 3 ingredients to a simmer in a saucepan, and cook, stirring occasionally, 6 minutes or until sugar dissolves and orange juice is reduced by half.
2. Remove from heat, and cool 15 minutes. Cover and chill until ready to use, or refrigerate in an airtight container up to 4 days.
3. Whisk together milk and next 3 ingredients in a saucepan over medium-low heat, and cook, whisking occasionally, 2 to 3 minutes or until sugar dissolves. Remove from heat.
4. Whisk together egg yolks and next 2 ingredients in a medium bowl until smooth. Gradually whisk ½ cup milk mixture into egg yolk mixture, whisking constantly until smooth. Pour yolk mixture into warm milk mixture in pan, whisking until blended. Cook over medium-high heat, whisking constantly, 3 to 5 minutes or until mixture thickens and begins to bubble.
5. Transfer to a bowl, and place plastic wrap directly on mixture (to prevent a film from forming). Chill 30 minutes to 3 days.
6. Cut pound cake into 1-inch cubes. Layer one-third cake cubes in a 2.5-qt. trifle dish. Top with one-third each orange pastry cream, cranberry mixture, and whipped cream. Repeat layers twice. Serve immediately, or cover and chill up to 24 hours. Garnish, if desired.

Note: We tested with Sara Lee All Butter Pound Cake.

Red Berry Pavlova Tower

Layer and fill this meringue turret up to one hour before serving
for the best contrast of crunchy, chewy, and creamy textures.

MAKES: 10 TO 12 SERVINGS HANDS-ON: 40 MIN. TOTAL: 4 HOURS 20 MIN., INCLUDING ICING

2 cups sugar	Parchment paper
2 Tbsp. cornstarch	Cheesecake Icing (recipe below)
8 large egg whites, at room temperature	Sweetened whipped cream
½ tsp. cream of tartar	2 lb. assorted fresh red berries (such as sliced strawberries and raspberries)
¼ tsp. table salt	
½ tsp. almond extract	Garnish: fresh mint sprigs

1. Preheat oven to 225°. Whisk together sugar and cornstarch. Beat egg whites at medium-high speed with a heavy-duty electric stand mixer, using whisk attachment, 1 minute; add cream of tartar and salt, beating until blended. Add sugar mixture, 2 Tbsp. at a time, beating until mixture is glossy, stiff peaks form, and sugar dissolves. (Do not overbeat.) Beat in almond extract. Reserve 1 cup meringue.

2. Gently spread enough meringue onto a parchment paper-lined baking sheet to make a 10-inch round (about 1 to 1½ inches high). Repeat procedure twice on another parchment paper-lined baking sheet, making an 8-inch round and a 6-inch round. Make an indentation in center of each meringue to hold filling.

3. Spoon reserved 1 cup meringue into a large zip-top plastic freezer bag. Snip 1 corner of bag to make a small hole. Pipe meringue onto baking sheet next to 10-inch round to resemble a large chocolate kiss.

4. Bake at 225° for 1 hour and 30 minutes or until outsides have formed a crust. Turn oven off; let meringues stand in oven, with door closed, 2 to 10 hours.

5. Place 10-inch meringue on a serving plate. Fill indentation with the desired amount of Cheesecake Icing, whipped cream, and berries. Top with remaining meringue layers, icing, whipped cream, and berries. Top with kiss-shaped meringue. Garnish, if desired. Serve within 1 hour.

Cheesecake Icing

Creamy Cheesecake Icing contributes to the contrast of textures in our meringue turret dessert.

¼ cup butter	½ cup powdered sugar
1 (8-oz.) package cream cheese, softened	¼ tsp. table salt
½ cup sour cream	

Beat butter and softened cream cheese at medium speed with an electric mixer until smooth. Add sour cream; beat until smooth. Gradually add powdered sugar and salt; beat until well blended. Use immediately, or chill up to 48 hours. Makes about 3 cups.

Raspberry Panna Cotta

MAKES: **8 SERVINGS** HANDS-ON: **20 MIN.** TOTAL: **2 HOURS 20 MIN.**

1	(1-oz.) envelope unflavored gelatin	⅓	cup sugar
2	cups cold milk	1	Tbsp. vanilla extract
2	pt. fresh raspberries	¼	tsp. table salt
3	Tbsp. sugar	1½	cups heavy cream
2	Tbsp. fresh lemon juice	Garnishes: fresh rosemary sprigs,	
1	tsp. ground cardamom (optional)		fresh raspberries

1. Sprinkle gelatin over milk in a saucepan; let stand 5 minutes.
2. Meanwhile, place 3 raspberries in each of 8 (6-oz.) parfait glasses or jars. Mash together 3 Tbsp. sugar, 2 Tbsp. lemon juice, remaining raspberries, and, if desired, cardamom in a medium bowl. Spoon 1 Tbsp. mashed raspberry mixture into each parfait glass. Reserve remaining berry mixture.
3. Stir ⅓ cup sugar, vanilla, and salt into milk mixture in saucepan, and cook over low heat, stirring constantly, 3 minutes or until sugar dissolves and milk begins to steam. Remove from heat; stir in cream. Pour milk mixture over raspberries in parfait glasses (about ½ cup per glass). Chill 2 hours or until firm. Top parfaits with reserved mashed raspberry mixture just before serving. Garnish, if desired.

Cardamom spice gives this silky custard its holiday flavor. Use any berry you wish, adjusting the sugar in the mixture to taste.

Charlotte Russe

MAKES: 8 TO 10 SERVINGS   HANDS-ON: 45 MIN.   TOTAL: 11 HOURS

1	(1-oz.) envelope unflavored gelatin
½	cup cold water
5	large egg yolks
1½	cups sugar
2	tsp. all-purpose flour
½	tsp. table salt
2	cups half-and-half
1	tsp. vanilla extract
½	cup dry sherry, divided
2	(3.5-oz.) packages ladyfinger biscotti
2	cups heavy cream

Garnishes: sweetened whipped cream, chocolate shavings, mandarin orange segments

1. Sprinkle gelatin over ½ cup cold water; stir and let stand 5 minutes. Whisk together egg yolks and next 3 ingredients in a bowl.

2. Bring half-and-half to a simmer in a medium saucepan over medium heat. Whisk ¼ cup hot half-and-half into egg mixture; add egg mixture to remaining hot half-and-half, whisking constantly. Reduce heat to medium-low, and cook, stirring constantly, 8 to 10 minutes or until mixture thickens and coats a spoon. Add vanilla, gelatin mixture, and ¼ cup sherry, stirring until combined.

3. Remove from heat; let stand 15 minutes. Transfer to a bowl. Cover and chill 2 hours or until mixture is a pudding-like thickness, stirring every 30 minutes.

4. Arrange 23 ladyfingers in a single layer on a jelly-roll pan. Brush both sides of ladyfingers with remaining ¼ cup sherry.

5. Line a 9-cup charlotte mold or soufflé dish with plastic wrap, allowing 2 to 3 inches to extend over sides. Line sides of mold with ladyfingers.

6. Beat cream at medium speed with a heavy-duty electric stand mixer 2 to 3 minutes or until soft peaks form. Fold whipped cream into chilled half-and-half mixture. Gently pour mixture into prepared charlotte mold. Cover and chill 8 to 24 hours or until fully set. To unmold, invert a flat plate over dessert. Holding containers together, invert. Lift off mold, and gently remove plastic wrap. Garnish, if desired. Cut dessert into wedges.

Note: We tested with Natural Nectar Biscotti Savoiardi Lady Fingers.

Chill any remaining custard, and serve it with the remaining ladyfingers for dipping.

HOLIDAY GIFTS

Show them that you love them by picking and choosing from these handmade, from-the-heart gifts for everyone on your list

FOR THE

Southern Baker

A decadent fudge filling gives bakers a shortcut to pie nirvana, while easy, homemade self-rising flour with cornmeal gives biscuits added texture.

MAKE THESE:
Hot Fudge Pie
MAKES: 1 (9-inch) pie
HANDS-ON: 5 min.
TOTAL: 1 hour 5 min., including filling

Hot Fudge Pie Filling: Microwave 1 cup half-and-half, ¼ cup butter, and 8 oz. chopped bittersweet chocolate in a microwave-safe bowl at HIGH 2 minutes or until chocolate melts. Stir until smooth. Stir together 1½ cups sugar, ¾ cup unsweetened cocoa, ¼ cup all-purpose flour, and ¼ tsp. table salt in a medium bowl. Stir in 2 large eggs, 3 large egg yolks, and melted chocolate mixture. Use immediately, or pour filling into a 1-qt. jar; let cool. Store filling in refrigerator up to 7 days. (Mixture will thicken as it chills.)

To Make Hot Fudge Pie: Preheat oven to 350°. Fit 1 refrigerated piecrust into a lightly greased 9-inch deep-dish pie plate according to package directions; fold edges under, and crimp. Pour Hot Fudge Pie Filling into prepared crust; bake 45 minutes or until filling puffs, center is set, and top begins to crack around the edges. Cool 10 minutes before serving.

Homemade Self-Rising Cornmeal Flour
MAKES: 3½ cups
HANDS-ON: 5 min.
TOTAL: 5 min.

Stir together 3 cups all-purpose flour, ⅓ cup plain yellow cornmeal, 4 tsp. baking powder, and 1 tsp. table salt. Place in a zip-top plastic freezer bag, and seal. Freeze up to 4 weeks.

To Use the Flour: Replace self-rising flour in any recipe (such as biscuits) with this cornmeal-enriched home-made version.

PACKAGE THEM IN:
Party treat boxes; Weck tall 28.7-oz. glass jars

FOR THE

Caramel Connoisseur

MAKE THESE:
Homemade Caramel Taffy
MAKES: 32 pieces
HANDS-ON: 35 min.
TOTAL: 2 hours 35 min.

Line bottom and sides of an 8-inch square pan with aluminum foil, allowing 2 to 3 inches to extend over sides. Generously grease foil. Melt 1 cup butter in a 3-qt. saucepan over low heat. Stir in 1 (16-oz.) package dark brown sugar, 1 (14-oz.) can sweetened condensed milk, and 1 cup light corn syrup until smooth. Bring to a boil. Cook over medium heat, stirring constantly, until a candy thermometer registers 235° (about 20 minutes). Remove from heat. Add 1 Tbsp. loosely packed orange zest; stir 1 minute or until mixture is smooth and no longer bubbling. Quickly pour into prepared pan. Let stand 2 hours. Lift caramels from pan, using foil sides as handles. Cut into 2- x 1-inch pieces with a buttered knife. Store at room temperature up to 1 week. To package for gifting, wrap each piece in a taffy wrapper.

Boozy Caramel Fudge
MAKES: 1 (9-inch) pan
HANDS-ON: 30 min.
TOTAL: 2 hours 45 min.

Line a 9-inch square pan with parchment paper; grease paper. Bring ¾ cup sugar, ¼ cup water, and 1 Tbsp. fresh lemon juice to a boil in a small saucepan over medium-high heat. Boil 8 to 10 minutes or until sugar begins to brown. (Do not stir.) Stir in ⅓ cup heavy cream and 2 Tbsp. butter; remove from heat. Stir constantly, until no longer bubbling. Microwave 2 (14-oz.) cans sweetened condensed milk and 2 (12-oz.) packages semisweet chocolate morsels in a large microwave-safe bowl at HIGH 3 minutes, stirring at 1-minute intervals. Stir in ¼ cup dark rum, 2½ Tbsp. butter, and ¼ tsp. table salt. Pour into prepared pan. Pour caramel over chocolate mixture; gently swirl with a knife. Chill 2 to 4 hours. Cut into pieces; wrap in wax paper. Refrigerate in an airtight container up to 1 week.

PACKAGE THEM IN:
Mini gingham cupcake liners; medium glassine bags

FOR THE
Cocktail Cognoscenti

Show them you're right on trend with a spirited olive garnish and versatile infused simple syrup.

MAKE THESE:
Lemon Simple Syrup
MAKES: 4 jars
HANDS-ON: 15 min.
TOTAL: 55 min.

Split 1 vanilla bean; scrape seeds into a saucepan. Place bean in pan; add 3 cups sugar, 2 cups water, and 6 lemons, sliced. Bring to a boil over medium heat. Reduce heat to low, and simmer, stirring occasionally, 10 minutes. Remove from heat; let stand 5 minutes. Pour through a fine wire-mesh strainer into a bowl; discard solids. Cool completely. Pour mixture into 4 (8-oz.) jars. Cover with lids. Store in refrigerator up to 3 weeks.

To Use the Syrup: Add to gin, vodka, or bourbon cocktails; iced tea; or lemonade.

Naughty Olives
MAKES: 4 jars
HANDS-ON: 35 min.
TOTAL: 4 hours 35 min.

Cook 2 tsp. fennel seeds, ½ tsp. black peppercorns, and ¼ tsp. dried crushed red pepper in a small saucepan over medium heat, stirring constantly, 1 to 2 minutes or until fragrant and lightly toasted. Add ½ cup liquid from jarred Spanish olives, 4 bay leaves, 4 (3-inch) orange peel strips, and 1 (6-inch) fresh rosemary sprig, and bring to a boil. Remove from heat, and add 1 cup extra-dry vermouth. Combine 3 cups drained Spanish olives and 1 cup drained cocktail onions in a medium bowl; spoon into 4 (8-oz.) jars. Place 1 bay leaf and 1 orange peel strip from vermouth mixture in each jar, and fill with vermouth mixture. Cover with lids. Chill 4 hours before serving. Store in refrigerator up to 3 weeks.

To Use the Olives: Serve as a cocktail garnish or bar snack.

PACKAGE THEM IN:
Weck short 9.8-oz. glass jars; cork Boston glass bottles

FOR THE
Brunch Bunch

Which came first, the chicken or the waffle? Decide over a brunch of pecan-crusted chicken tenders with a bacon-studded waffle.

MAKE THESE:
Pecan-Cornmeal Dredge
MAKES: 5½ cups
HANDS-ON: 15 min.
TOTAL: 15 min.

Stir together 2 cups coarsely chopped pecans, 2 cups all-purpose flour, 1 cup plain yellow cornmeal, ½ cup chopped shallots, 1 Tbsp. kosher salt, 1 Tbsp. chopped fresh rosemary, and 1 tsp. freshly ground black pepper in a large bowl. Refrigerate in an airtight container up to 1 week.

Pecan Chicken Tenders
MAKES: 4 servings
HANDS-ON: 35 min.
TOTAL: 35 min.

Place Pecan-Cornmeal Dredge in a shallow bowl. Whisk together 1 large egg and ½ cup milk in another shallow bowl. Dip 16 chicken breast tenders, 1 at a time, in egg mixture; dredge in Pecan-Cornmeal Dredge. Pour vegetable oil to depth of 2 inches into a Dutch oven; heat to 325°. Fry chicken, in batches, in hot oil 5 to 6 minutes or until done. Drain on a wire rack over paper towels.

Bacon Waffle Mix
MAKES: 8 (4-inch) waffles (about ½ cup batter per waffle)
HANDS-ON: 35 min.
TOTAL: 35 min.

Whisk together 2 cups all-purpose flour, 2 Tbsp. sugar, 1 Tbsp. baking powder, ½ tsp. kosher salt, and 5 cooked and crumbled bacon slices. Refrigerate in an airtight container up to 1 week.

To Make Bacon Waffles: Place Bacon Waffle Mix in a medium bowl; stir in 1¼ cups milk, ¼ cup melted butter, and 2 large eggs. Cook in a preheated oiled waffle iron until done.

PACKAGE THEM IN:
Party treat boxes; Weck tall 28.7-oz. glass jars

FOR THE

Cheese Lover

Update the cheese platter with a new cheese ball,
spiced honey for drizzling, and marinated feta.

MAKE THESE:
Smoky Cheese Ball
MAKES: I cheese ball
HANDS-ON: I5 min.
TOTAL: 25 min.

Cook 6 hickory-smoked bacon slices in a skillet over medium heat 5 to 8 minutes or until crisp; remove bacon, reserving 2 Tbsp. drippings in skillet. Crumble bacon. Sauté ½ cup chopped pecans in hot drippings 2 minutes. Cool I0 minutes. Stir together 2 cups (8 oz.) freshly shredded sharp Cheddar cheese, ⅓ cup mayonnaise, ¼ cup sliced green onions, ½ tsp. kosher salt, ¼ tsp. ground red pepper, 3 oz. softened cream cheese, bacon, and pecans. Shape into a ball. Wrap in plastic wrap.

Lemony Garlic
Feta Cheese
MAKES: I pt.
HANDS-ON: I5 min.
TOTAL: I5 min., plus I day for chilling

Heat I cup olive oil and 3 smashed garlic cloves in a saucepan over medium-low heat 2 to 3 minutes or until garlic starts to bubble. Remove from heat, and cool completely. Layer 2 oz. feta cheese, cubed; 2 lemon slices; 4 small fresh thyme sprigs; and ¼ cup Castelvetrano olives in I (I-pt.) jar. Repeat layers once. Pour oil-garlic mixture into jar. Add additional oil to fill jar. Cover and chill 24 hours before serving.

Chile-Infused Honey
MAKES: I ⅓ cups
HANDS-ON: I0 min.
TOTAL: I2 hours 55 min.

Stir together I cup honey; ½ tsp. dried crushed red pepper; ¼ tsp. kosher salt; 2 fresh peppers (such as serrano or jalapeño), sliced; and I (4-inch) fresh rosemary sprig in a saucepan. Cook over medium heat 2 to 3 minutes. Remove from heat; cool completely. Spoon into I (8-oz.) jar. Chill I2 to 24 hours. Store in refrigerator up to 2 weeks. Let stand at room temperature 30 minutes before serving.

PACKAGE THEM IN:
Glass canisters with wood or cork lids

FOR THE

Italophile

Spiced nuts make a great stir-in for pasta;
roasted sweet peppers, a sweet bruschetta topper.

MAKE THESE:
Garlicky Mixed Nuts
MAKES: 6 to 8 servings
HANDS-ON: I0 min.
TOTAL: I0 min.

Cook ½ cup chopped pecans and ¼ cup each pine nuts, sliced almonds, and blanched hazelnuts in ⅓ cup hot olive oil in a medium skillet over medium heat, stirring constantly, 2 minutes or until toasted. Remove from heat. Stir in ½ cup chopped fresh flat-leaf parsley, ⅓ cup golden raisins, 2 tsp. chopped fresh thyme, I tsp. loosely packed orange zest, ½ tsp. dried crushed red pepper, ¼ tsp. table salt, and I large garlic clove, sliced. Pour mixture into I (8-oz.) jar. Store in refrigerator up to 2 weeks.

To Make Pasta With Garlic Nuts: Cook Garlicky Mixed Nuts in 2 Tbsp. hot olive oil in a medium skillet over medium heat I to 2 minutes or until fragrant. Toss with I6 oz. hot cooked pasta. Serve immediately with grated Parmesan cheese.

Roasted Sweet Peppers
MAKES: I pt.
HANDS-ON: I5 min.
TOTAL: 40 min.

Preheat oven to 450°. Toss together I ½ lb. sweet mini bell peppers; 3 garlic cloves, unpeeled; and 2 Tbsp. olive oil. Bake in a single layer in a jelly-roll pan 25 to 30 minutes or until peppers look blistered, stirring every I0 minutes. Peel, seed, and coarsely chop peppers. Peel and slice garlic; stir into peppers. Stir in ¼ cup torn fresh basil, 2 Tbsp. chopped fresh chives, I tsp. loosely packed lemon zest, ¾ tsp. kosher salt, and ½ tsp. dried crushed red pepper. Spoon into I (I-pt.) jar. Store in refrigerator up to I week.

To Use Roasted Sweet Peppers: Spoon over toasted French bread slices, or serve on a cheese tray.

PACKAGE THEM IN:
Weck short 9.8-oz. and I2.5-oz. glass jars

FOR THE
Lowcountry Lover

*Break out the propane cooker and a big pot
for a Lowcountry boil spiced with this mix.*

MAKE THESE:
Carolina Mustard Sauce
MAKES: I (8-oz.) jar
HANDS-ON: 5 min.
TOTAL: 5 min.

Stir together ½ cup mayonnaise, ½ cup Dijon mustard, 2 tsp. Worcestershire sauce, and I Tbsp. Asian hot chili sauce (such as Sriracha) in a small bowl. Spoon mustard sauce into I (8-oz.) jar. Store in refrigerator up to 3 weeks.

Note: We tested with Maille Dijon Originale Mustard.

Shrimp-and-Crab Boil Sachets
MAKES: 2 sachets
HANDS-ON: 5 min.
TOTAL: 15 min.

Place 2 (8-inch-square) triple layers of cheesecloth on a flat surface. Heat 3 Tbsp. black peppercorns, 3 Tbsp. coriander seeds, 2 Tbsp. dried crushed red pepper, 2 Tbsp. mustard seeds, I Tbsp. dill seeds, I Tbsp. celery seeds, and 3 crushed bay leaves in a hot skillet over medium-high heat, stirring constantly, I to 2 minutes or until fragrant. Cool 10 minutes. Stir in ¼ cup kosher salt. Divide mixture between 2 cheesecloth stacks. Gather edges of cheesecloth together; tie with kitchen string. Store at room temperature up to 2 weeks. For gifting, package each sachet with 3 lemons, 2 yellow onions, and 2 garlic bulbs.

Boiled Shrimp
MAKES: 6 servings
HANDS-ON: 15 min.
TOTAL: I hr., 5 min.

Bring 6 cups water; 3 lemons, sliced; 2 yellow onions, sliced; 2 garlic bulbs; and I Shrimp-and-Crab Boil Sachet to a boil in a large Dutch oven over medium-high heat; boil 30 minutes. Add 3 lb. unpeeled, large raw shrimp; cover and remove from heat. Let stand 10 minutes or just until shrimp turn pink. Discard sachet, and serve boiled shrimp with Carolina Mustard Sauce.

PACKAGE THEM IN:
Weck short 9.8-oz. glass jars

FOR THE
Backyard Grillmaster

*Fire up his or her imagination with an
all-purpose BBQ rub and sweet-and-sticky sauce.*

MAKE THESE:
Smoky Grill Rub
MAKES: I (8-oz.) jar
HANDS-ON: 5 min.
TOTAL: 5 min.

Stir together 3 Tbsp. sweet paprika, 3 Tbsp. ground cumin, 2 Tbsp. kosher salt, 2 Tbsp. dark brown sugar, I Tbsp. smoked paprika, 2½ tsp. ground red pepper, 1½ tsp. garlic powder, and I tsp. celery seeds. Spoon rub into an 8-oz. jar or container, and store at room temperature.

To Use Rub: Sprinkle or rub it on chicken, pork, or any full-flavored fish, such as salmon, before grilling.

Sweet Tomato Barbecue Sauce
MAKES: 3 (8-oz.) containers
HANDS-ON: 10 min.
TOTAL: 2 hours 30 min.

Drain I (28-oz.) can whole peeled plum tomatoes, and crush tomatoes. Melt ¼ cup butter in a small saucepan over medium-high heat. Add 1½ cups coarsely chopped yellow onion, and sauté 3 minutes. Add 4 smashed garlic cloves, and sauté I minute. Stir ½ cup sugar, ½ cup cider vinegar, ¼ cup white vinegar, 2 Tbsp. tomato paste, 2 tsp. kosher salt, 2 tsp. Worcestershire sauce, I tsp. freshly ground black pepper, and crushed tomatoes into onion mixture; bring to a boil. Reduce heat to low; simmer, stirring occasionally, 2 hours or until color is deep red and most of liquid has evaporated. Remove from heat, and let mixture stand 15 minutes. Process mixture in a blender or food processor until smooth. Spoon into 3 (8-oz.) glass containers. Store barbecue sauce in refrigerator up to 3 weeks.

PACKAGE THEM IN:
Round spice jars; square swingtop 8.5-oz. bottles

Metric Equivalents

The recipes that appear in this cookbook use the standard United States method for measuring liquid and dry or solid ingredients (teaspoons, tablespoons, and cups). The information in the following charts is provided to help cooks outside the U.S. successfully use these recipes. All equivalents are approximate.

Metric Equivalents for Different Types of Ingredients

A standard cup measure of a dry or solid ingredient will vary in weight depending on the type of ingredient. A standard cup of liquid is the same volume for any type of liquid. Use the following chart when converting standard cup measures to grams (weight) or milliliters (volume).

Standard Cup	Fine Powder (ex. flour)	Grain (ex. rice)	Granular (ex. sugar)	Liquid Solids (ex. butter)	Liquid (ex. milk)
1	140 g	150 g	190 g	200 g	240 ml
¾	105 g	113 g	143 g	150 g	180 ml
⅔	93 g	100 g	125 g	133 g	160 ml
½	70 g	75 g	95 g	100 g	120 ml
⅓	47 g	50 g	63 g	67 g	80 ml
¼	35 g	38 g	48 g	50 g	60 ml
⅛	18 g	19 g	24 g	25 g	30 ml

Useful Equivalents for Dry Ingredients by Weight

(To convert ounces to grams, multiply the number of ounces by 30.)

1 oz	=	¹⁄₁₆ lb	=	30 g
4 oz	=	¼ lb	=	120 g
8 oz	=	½ lb	=	240 g
12 oz	=	¾ lb	=	360 g
16 oz	=	1 lb	=	480 g

Useful Equivalents for Length

(To convert inches to centimeters, multiply the number of inches by 2.5.)

1 in				=	2.5 cm	
6 in	=	½ ft		=	15 cm	
12 in	=	1 ft		=	30 cm	
36 in	=	3 ft	= 1 yd	=	90 cm	
40 in				=	100 cm	= 1 m

Useful Equivalents for Liquid Ingredients by Volume

¼ tsp						=	1 ml	
½ tsp						=	2 ml	
1 tsp						=	5 ml	
3 tsp	=	1 Tbsp			= ½ fl oz	=	15 ml	
		2 Tbsp	=	⅛ cup	= 1 fl oz	=	30 ml	
		4 Tbsp	=	¼ cup	= 2 fl oz	=	60 ml	
		5⅓ Tbsp	=	⅓ cup	= 3 fl oz	=	80 ml	
		8 Tbsp	=	½ cup	= 4 fl oz	=	120 ml	
		10⅔ Tbsp	=	⅔ cup	= 5 fl oz	=	160 ml	
		12 Tbsp	=	¾ cup	= 6 fl oz	=	180 ml	
		16 Tbsp	=	1 cup	= 8 fl oz	=	240 ml	
		1 pt	=	2 cups	= 16 fl oz	=	480 ml	
		1 qt	=	4 cups	= 32 fl oz	=	960 ml	
					33 fl oz	=	1000 ml	= 1 l

Useful Equivalents for Cooking/Oven Temperatures

	Fahrenheit	Celsius	Gas Mark
Freeze water	32° F	0° C	
Room temperature	68° F	20° C	
Boil water	212° F	100° C	
Bake	325° F	160° C	3
	350° F	180° C	4
	375° F	190° C	5
	400° F	200° C	6
	425° F	220° C	7
	450° F	230° C	8
Broil			Grill

General Index

Recipe Index

Senior Editor: Katherine Cobbs
Editor: Susan Ray
Assistant Project Editors: Kylie Dazzo, Dree Deacon
Art Director: Christopher Rhoads
Junior Designer: AnnaMaria Jacob
Executive Photography Director: Iain Bagwell
Assistant Production Director: Sue Chodakiewicz
Senior Production Manager: Greg Amason
Copy Editor: Jasmine Hodges
Proofreaders: Lauren Brooks, Adrienne Davis

ISBN 13: 978-0-8487-4549-3
ISBN 10: 0-8487-4549-3
Library of Congress Control Number: 2015950560

Printed in the United States of America

10 9 8 7 6 5 4 3 2 1

First Printing 2015